The Woman's Day Guide to Organizing Your Life

·THE·
WOMAN'S DAY
GUIDE TO
ORGANIZING
YOUR LIFE

❖ ❖ ❖ ❖ ❖

DIANE HARRIS

An Owl Book
Holt, Rinehart and Winston / New York

I'd like to thank all the people at Owl Books for their outstanding editorial help, patience, and encouragement.

To Serge

Contents

The
Woman's Day
Guide to
Organizing
Your Life

· 1 · Getting Started at Getting Organized

Life is a lot more satisfying when you're organized. Everything goes more smoothly. You work more effectively, learn more easily, and play with great exuberance when you're not distracted by disorder, worried about unpaid bills, or pressured by unrealistic schedules. When you organize your time and your money, both seem to grow as if by magic. When you get your papers in order, you eliminate hours of frustrated searching. When you organize your housework and your kitchen, you get twice as much done in half the time. It isn't a matter of fanatical neatness, it's knowing what your priorities are and how to do what's important to you as efficiently as possible.

Knowing this, why is it that so many of us still have trouble getting organized? Why does the thought of tackling our tangled money matters, messy papers, and cluttered closets inspire gloom and discouragement in the hearts of otherwise sensible and energetic people? Is there hope for all those who feel convinced they were born disorganized? What does it take to go from world-class chaotic to ordinary orderliness?

Well, the good news is that there are organizational skills you can learn. And as soon as you put them into practice in the problem areas of your life, you'll see dramatic improvement. But it's not a onetime thing. You'll have to introduce a periodic review to make sure you don't get sidetracked as you add new activities and as your goals change. One reason many of us find ourselves in a state of disorganization is that we've carried over a system that worked well in one phase of our lives into a new and different phase where it's inappropriate. A casual attitude toward money and budgeting may have been fine when you were single, but it just won't work now that you're married and have a child. Or maybe you'd worked out a reasonably efficient housekeeping system while you were at home with your kids, but now that you're back at work, you're plagued by dust balls in the living room, dishes in the sink, and a kitchen floor your mother would have considered a capital offense. Confronted with a breakdown in an old system and a buildup of new problems, many of us feel stymied. We're not sure what our first move should be. It's tempting just to clean up the surface disorder and leave the underlying confusion pretty much the same. But superficial improvements will just postpone the day of reckoning. The problems are sure to surface again. And our sense of competence takes a beating.

Another important reason many of us don't attack the source of the problems is that we often don't have enough information or technical know-how to really solve the problem. Think for a minute about the area of finances. Obviously you can't organize your money if you don't know how to plan a budget, what guidelines the experts recommend for wise credit use, or what the best savings approach would be to achieve your short-term and long-term goals. You need hard facts.

A Strategy for Change

Whatever the reason or reasons for your not being as organized as you want to be, the system offered in this book will show you how to bypass procrastination, get to the root of your problem, and develop a personalized plan that will give you the order you want. And the strategy provides built-in monitoring that helps to make sure things don't go really haywire again.

Each of the chapters that follow is devoted to a different important area of life—time, money, papers, housekeeping, the kitchen, storage, shopping, children, and entertaining and holidays—and each utilizes the following four-point strategy for getting the areas under control:

1. *Instant-Action Step.* A quick corrective measure that provides immediate relief, introduces a systematic approach, and lays the groundwork for more thoroughgoing long-term improvements.

2. *In-Depth Assessment.* Simple techniques for making a point-by-point analysis of the area under consideration to help establish priorities, pinpoint stumbling blocks, and keep the big picture in focus.

3. *Personalized Organization Plan.* Proven tactics to solve the problems you've identified (or always knew about) and to achieve the goals you and your family have set.

4. *Regular Reevaluation.* Procedures to help you stay on target or shift gears gracefully, including an Annual Review (right after New Year's is an ideal time) to monitor your situation and prevent backsliding, and a quick Spot-Check Review to cope with any situation that may be getting out of control.

The techniques offered here have been carefully designed to allow you to bypass the most common forms of procrastination and to move forward at a satisfying pace to correct basic underlying problems. In each chapter, tactics are tailored to suit the requirements of the area under attack, yet the same basic approach is used in every case. And you can apply it to areas outside the scope of this book, such as school and work. Throughout, the emphasis is on breaking big jobs into manageable segments and making sure that each succeeding section builds on what has gone before. By creating a written master plan, you'll know exactly how to proceed. And the Instant-Action Step allows you to get moving right away and achieve clear-cut results even in normally resistant areas. For best results, it's a good idea to read through each chapter completely, maybe even more than once, and then dig in. But before you even begin to get organized, here are a few important things to bear in mind.

Start Small for Success

Very often when people make a decision to get organized it's because things have gotten so badly out of control that they feel the need for drastic corrective action. In that frame of mind it's easy to convince yourself that the best approach is an all-out assault on your big problems—taking everything out of the hall closet before you know what you're going to do with it, confining yourself to a pennypincher's allowance, reorganizing your desk and everything in it. Yet tempting as such extreme actions are, they're almost always the wrong thing to do. It's similar to going on a crash diet. You can't correct months or years of neglect and confusion with one day's efforts. And when you try that approach, you'll probably get deeper into confusion, feel messier than ever, and get badly discouraged. Only if your mother-in-law is coming to visit you from Spokane in a few days or the IRS is scheduled to arrive for an at-home audit should you consider an onslaught approach. In such serious cases, extreme measures are justified, despite the toll it may take on your mental and physical state. But as a general rule, you're much more likely to succeed if you start small, proceed at a comfortable pace, and do a really thorough job.

Begin by choosing the area you consider your most pressing problem, read the relevant chapter through, and then take the Instant-Action Step in that chapter. Or you might find it more useful to read Chapter 2, Making the Most of Your Time, to get a clearer idea of your priorities and how to schedule your activities. And move through the chapter in sequence. Whatever you decide to do, devote only one hour to it and then schedule additional work sessions for the coming weeks. Mark the sessions on your calendar, and consider them fixed and crucial and just keep working until you've completed the job. One day at a time you can correct even colossal problems and soon see noticeable improvement. And as you move forward from area to area, you'll find that you have a momentum inspired by your continued successes to get your whole life in smooth-functioning order.

Realistic Expectations

Often, when we have fantasies about being organized, the picture we see in our mind's eye is a polished, perfectly ordered world with rooms so immaculate they could be featured in an architectural magazine, closets and cabinets so tidy they could be opened for public inspection, and ourselves coolly overseeing the whole scene and wonderfully put together in every respect. In short, we have visions of perfection. And when we find ourselves back in the real world, it can come as a shock to recognize that reality isn't like that. Keeping that kind of ideal as a goal can be a serious stumbling block to getting started.

And the truth is that only rooms in museums or historic houses or model apartments look like that. It's not only impossible to achieve such extraordinary neatness, I'm not even sure it's desirable. If you were to encounter such perfection in real life—and it occasionally happens—you'd probably feel uncomfortable because you couldn't relax, ignore your surroundings, and get on with living. The best approach to organization is to think of it as a means toward a more pleasurable and rewarding life. If you see it as a way of life rather than some final end point, you'll have more realistic expectations of yourself and your family and you'll free yourself to accomplish much more than when you cling to perfectionistic standards.

Very few people are as organized as they want to be. Even the great statesman/inventor/writer Benjamin Franklin had problems getting his schedule and possessions under control. In fact, he wrote in his autobiography, "In truth, I felt myself incorrigible with respect to order. . . . " Now, considering all that Franklin achieved, it may come as quite a surprise that he could view himself in such a critical light. Clearly he had pretty exacting standards. One vital lesson we can take away from his story is that all people, no matter how gifted, who are busy living fully, creating, and contributing to their societies, are bound to produce a certain amount of disorder and upheaval. To stay constantly immaculately neat may restrict our creative impulses.

Coping with Special Situations

No one book can cover every single aspect of the problems you may be confronting in organizing your life. Different people have different needs. If, for example, you have to get up at dawn to commute to your job, you won't have time for morning chores at home. If you have two preschoolers under five, you'll have to schedule your activities around their naps, activities, and sessions in their playgroup. If you're running a catering or baking business out of your home, you'll have to plan, cook, and perhaps freeze family meals to avoid conflicts. What the Four-Point Strategy is designed to do is show you a method for resolving problems in any area that's important to you.

Allowing for the Unexpected

Sometimes when we're in the middle of a transition and putting new tactics into practice—new morning schedules, new mealtime job assignments, new shopping techniques—we have the feeling that we've just barely established a beachhead and we can easily fall back into the sea. Feeling somewhat insecure, we might get temporarily overwrought. If you've just put the finishing touches on a gleaming living-room cleanup, you can get pretty disturbed if somebody comes along and puts a newspaper on the couch. Or if your daughter comes home too late to set the table because of a tie-up at her band rehearsal, you can get very agitated. If you start feeling and acting like a top sergeant inspecting the barracks, you'll defeat the purpose of your efforts, which was to make life pleasanter and more productive. Life is not predictable. Changes are going to occur, accidents are going to happen, and unexpected visitors are going to arrive. And since it's change that adds richness and interest to life, try to stay relaxed enough to enjoy the surprises when they're pleasant and to keep your perspective when they're not. A sense of humor is absolutely essential.

Celebrate Your Successes

The real rewards of organizing your life are that you feel better about yourself and you get to do more of the things that really matter to you. It's especially satisfying to feel capable and productive again. But while you're in the middle of the reformation process you may begin to feel that life is all work and no play. It can look like a never-ending ordeal. The best way to avoid such moods and see yourself through the low points is to check off jobs as you accomplish them and make sure you celebrate your successes along the way. Brag a bit to a friend who will congratulate you. Buy yourself a small gift—maybe a few flowers for your living room when you get it in shape or a new houseplant for your bedroom. Or take a day off and do just what you want to do. Also, remember to offer generous praise to other family members when they contribute to the reorganization plans. And giving a special treat is a nice idea as well. If you keep a positive attitude and proceed confidently, step by step you'll soon be organized.

· 2 · | Making the Most of Your Time

One dictionary definition of time is "an opportunity." And learning to manage your time wisely will give you opportunities in abundance. You'll be able to live life to the fullest. It isn't a matter of squeezing in as many activities as you can each day. It's finding out what's important to you and making sure you focus on these things. And it involves discovering the right balance between work and play, family time and private time, physical activity and mental pursuits, and efforts for short-term and long-term goals. It's when we lose sight of balance that we generally get into trouble. But achieving sound time management is an individual matter. What may be hard work for you can be relaxation for others.

How is it possible to get to the point where you're not sure what your goals are and whether you're doing the right things to achieve them? Well, sometimes it happens because we've moved to a new phase in life—perhaps our children are in high school and we could go back to work or school as we had hoped but we're locked into old ways of doing things. Or maybe we just continue to do things we once enjoyed but don't any longer—seeing people we don't really enjoy or helping out a friend who has a catering service—because it's easier than stopping and changing. Or maybe we just haven't given ourselves the time recently to really think about what we want for ourselves. It's a process we have to do every year or two. And it requires self-searching and often some hard choices. Because despite what some writers may claim, it really isn't possible to have it all. You only have so much time and you'll have to decide what really matters so you can allocate it wisely. So if you want satisfying relationships, meaningful work, and some fun in your life, you'll have to concentrate on the top priorities and downplay what's not important to you.

While it's true that we have to focus our energies on high-priority items, it's equally true that if we master the basic techniques of time management, we can do a great deal more every day than we would have thought possible. It's not just a matter of intelligent scheduling. It's learning to do most things with maximum efficiency and eliminating others altogether. This whole book is devoted to tactics and tips that will show you how to do that.

To learn exactly how you are spending your time, what the time wasters are, and what the remedies should be, you'll have to keep a log, an assessment of everything you do; and that will require at least a week's evaluation time. So if your scheduling problems have reached a state of emergency, you'll probably want an Instant-Action Step that will help you quickly introduce more order and serenity in your life. The best corrective measure I've found is the Night-Before Planning Notebook. Not only is this a great place to begin, it should become a permanent part of your time-management tactics. Another helpful interim measure will be reviewing the section later in this chapter on Solving the Ten Most Common Time Problems.

The Instant-Action Step—
Starting the Day Well

Often people who are very clear about needing to organize their time are not so clear about how to take the first step. When you're just starting out it's a bit like unraveling a tangled skein of yarn, so it makes sense to begin with one end of your day. And since mornings are characteristically the most jumbled time and usually set the tone for the rest of the day, they are a good place to begin. If you can eliminate the snags and snarls from your mornings, you're well on the way to more productive and satisfying days. Starting off smoothly increases your sense of competence and assurance, which is the best foundation for dealing with the remainder of the day.

Because many of us are too muddled in the morning to think clearly and react with flexibility, it often happens that when one thing goes wrong we suddenly find ourselves awash in confusion and irritability. Or we might find that everything goes smoothly until we're just about to leave the house and we discover that our car keys have mysteriously disappeared (and the duplicates are nowhere to be found) or it's the day of the Thanksgiving pageant and your daughter can't find her Indian headdress. Coping with such minor setbacks (or, better still, preventing them in the first place) is an easy matter if you've done a systematic review in your Night-Before Planning Notebook. By writing down everything you have to do, checking the family calendar for other important events, and getting ready in advance, you'll find that most problems never arise. And even if a mishap does occur, the planning you've done will help prevent a snowballing of troubles.

The Night-Before Planning Notebook

To begin using the system, here's all you do. Buy a notebook that's small enough to carry around with you. Set aside fifteen minutes every evening to plan your schedule for the following day. As I've suggested above, pay special attention to the early part of the morning. Begin by listing your usual trouble spots. Consider the problems listed below and then add your own particular dilemmas. Are any of these regular difficulties for you?

- Falling back to sleep after the alarm goes off
- Traffic pileup in the bathroom
- Problems choosing clothes
- Preparing breakfast takes too long
- Preparing brown-bag lunches takes too long

- Forgetting to take food for dinner out of freezer
- Forgetting to take items for repairs
- Forgetting to take sports equipment and gym clothes on days when you go to the gym
- Can't find watch, glasses, car keys

After you've written a problem in the Planning Notebook that you want to resolve, think about all the possible solutions. Let your imagination really go. For example, if you fall back to sleep after your alarm goes off, you could buy a clock radio with a "snooze" alarm that will allow you an extra fifteen minutes of sleep, or you could try going to bed a half-hour earlier, or you could get a time-controlled coffeemaker so that you would have coffee ready to drink the minute you got up. If you have clothes problems, you could make sure the night before that you have at least two outfits you could wear the next day—always have a couple of wash-and-wear knits for this purpose. If you can never find your keys, get a hook or a ceramic bowl to put near your front entrance and make it a rule to deposit your keys there every night. Don't settle for solutions that don't seem simple and practical. If you can't come up with something, ask for suggestions from your family. Choose only two or three of your problems to eliminate during the coming week. If you try to change too much at once, you're likely to backslide. Getting rid of old habits takes real effort. So let yourself get accustomed to doing just a few things a new way, then move on to other areas as you improve.

Once you've reviewed your usual morning difficulties, you're ready to write out a schedule for the next day with the corrective measures listed and underlined. Write your early-morning activities in the exact order you want to do them—with as little wasted motion as possible. The point is, you want to establish a comfortable routine that will become second nature to you in time. Allocate times to each activity, but don't schedule yourself so tightly that one small hitch will get you into trouble. No matter how well you prepare in advance, small mishaps or interruptions are going to occur. Build in a margin of about fifteen to twenty minutes.

The first day plan only your morning in this kind of detail. You can write out afternoon and evening activities in a broader way for the next two days. Concentrate on mornings, and mornings will start improving. Then you can expand your schedule to cover the whole day. Star any high-priority items. Use double stars next to any activity you can't postpone to another day.

At first, the Planning Notebook is used as an emergency device; as you get the knack of doing a full-fledged schedule, you'll discover ways to make it more and more useful. You can build in early holiday shopping, jot down the name of an interesting shop you hear about, start a list of parents to get in touch with for the school fair—whatever you'd like to take action on. It will not only help you meet daily responsibilities, but stimulate you to take preliminary steps in moving toward your long-term goals in the back of your book. But enter groundwork steps in your daily lists whenever they seem to make sense. For instance, if you'd like to take a computer course next because you've been thinking of buying a cheap one in a year or so, mark that down. Or if you've been meaning to get a brochure about a state park you think you want to visit, mark that on your daily list. If you want to find out more about CDs at your bank, for saving toward your kid's education, that too should be in your daily as well as your long-term lists. By keeping all of these lists in one place you'll be able to check back to see when you ordered a chair, when your child saw the doctor last, and lots of other important information. It's a basic time-management tool.

You won't be able to establish new short-term and long-term goals for yourself until you keep a Weekly Time Chart. But before you get started at that, it will probably be helpful to you to review some of the most common day-to-day time problems.

Solving the Ten Most Common Time Problems

Pacing is one secret of good time management—learning to work hard for a time and then give ourselves the benefit of a refreshing change of pace. As a result, most of the problems we have to deal with come about because we've gotten either too intense or too easygoing to maintain the right pace. Another source of difficulty is that we may keep adding new tasks and not eliminate any old ones until we just reach a point of crisis overload. Whatever your particular time-use problems are, you'll probably find them listed here along with some suggestions for overcoming them. By identifying the specific stumbling blocks you have to confront, you can begin to do something concrete about them. You may have been accusing yourself of procrastination or laziness when the real trouble is that you've overscheduled your time or haven't learned how to say no.

1. *Tackling too many jobs at once.* Doubling up and dovetailing jobs that are undemanding is highly recommended (for example, sewing on buttons when you make required phone calls); but most jobs require concentration.

Solution: Focus on one demanding job at a time so that you will function with maximum efficiency—and won't waste both time and energy dashing back and forth between two or more jobs.

2. *Underestimating how long things take.* If you continually underestimate the time it takes for jobs, the best way to establish sound scheduling practices is to start timing yourself at your chores. How long does your weekly shopping trip to the supermarket take? How long does it take to deep-clean the house—or the living room? Also, if you're not sure, build in some leeway.

Solution: Become familiar with the time it takes to perform your usual chores and remember to build in a margin of safety when you take on a new project—perhaps adding ten or fifteen minutes for a small job and a half hour for big jobs. To get yourself to time jobs, try pretending that you're a caterer or a professional housekeeper and you have to time your activities to guarantee that you make an appropriate income.

3. *Spending too much time on minor jobs.* If you find yourself turning into a perfectionist when you do small jobs, it may reflect the fact that you haven't evaluated your time and activities recently and haven't assigned a priority to them. Or you could be concentrating on easy little jobs to avoid a tough important one. Whenever you find yourself polishing glasses or kitchen counter-

tops to glistening perfection, stop and ask yourself, What are you avoiding?

Solution: If your difficulty arises because of lack of planning, you'll be better prepared to cope with this after you've done the Weekly Time Chart that appears later in this chapter. However, if you find that you're doing small things to avoid big ones, it may help if you break large jobs into manageable segments, and when you complete each one reward yourself. Schedule yourself as you alternate hard and easy chores.

4. *Not saying no when you want to.* It's easy to get into the habit of saying yes to requests from friends, family, and acquaintances because: (1) we don't stop to think whether we really want or have the time to do whatever it is; (2) we're flattered to be asked; (3) saying no might make people angry; (4) because we can't think of a good way to refuse.

Solution: Keep your priorities firmly in mind. Call to mind the situations in which you're most likely to agree to activities you don't want to do and decide how you could say no effectively. Write these down. Start noticing how other people handle similar situations. Create a list of explanations or excuses to use with people you know are going to call and make requests.

5. *Not setting deadlines.* Even if you have to meet deadlines set by others, it makes sense to begin setting your own deadlines for jobs and chores. Having no time limits encourages procrastination and too slow a pace.

Solution: If you set target completion times and dates for your jobs and projects, you'll get much more done. Break large projects into small segments and set a deadline for each segment. Mark deadlines on your personal calendar and, if it will help you, on the monthly calendar in the kitchen. Give yourself reasonable goals. If you ask the impossible of yourself you'll get discouraged and tense. Reasonable expectations encourage you to get things done and reap the benefits of productivity.

6. *Working too intensely without a break.* Often when we have an important or difficult job to do, we decide to concentrate on it and work steadily until we get it done. But this can lead to stress and inefficiency. Brain researchers have discovered that

people may think they're functioning well even after they have become tired and inefficient.

Solution: Take a break from any job every forty-five minutes or so. For relaxation do anything that appeals to you: listen to a favorite record; do something physical if you've been sitting quietly; or, vice versa, take a short walk for a change of scene. Or you might make a necessary phone call or do some brief chore in the kitchen. Change of pace is what you're after.

7. *Wasting travel and waiting time.* If you have a long commute to work or must make long drives anywhere often, it's easy to let those times become periods of mounting frustration or daydreaming. Waiting in lines at banks and supermarkets, waiting in doctors' and dentists' offices, waiting to pick up your kids, all of these can mount up and cause stress.

Solution: Think of ways to make your travel time less tense and frustrating. If you drive, take along tapes you like—of music, language lessons, great plays, whatever appeals to you. If you have to wait inside, have reading matter, your Planning Notebook, notepaper to write notes. When you're waiting at home for a repairman to come, for the kids to get ready, for a phone call, use the time to complete small tasks that you've grouped—do mending, sew on buttons, make phone calls, sketch out menus. Or if you've been rushing around, just relax for a bit and take a break.

8. *Indulging in too many time wasters.* If you don't guard against them, such activities as chatting with friends, watching your favorite soap operas, reading the newspaper word for word, can expand to fill the best part of the morning or afternoon.

Solution: Schedule a break to indulge one of these, but only after you've completed an important task. And use a timer to set reasonable limits for phone calls. Plan coffee breaks so that you can look forward to them as you work.

9. *Putting things off.* There are lots of reasons for procrastination. Sometimes we just don't like whatever job it is we have to do, and other times we're worried that we may not do it well enough to meet our own high standards—or someone else's.

Solution: One good way to get yourself moving is to write a list of all the positive results you'll get from accomplishing the job.

You can throw in negative consequences if you need even more incentive. Also, break the job down into portions you feel confident of doing pretty well and reward yourself when you complete each section. Another useful hint from the experts is to think about the job to find some aspect of it that you like, and begin with that. Getting started is the crucial step, so do whatever you must to get yourself to begin.

10. *Ignoring individual daily cycles of high-energy and low-energy periods.* Researchers have found that all of us have daily cycles of energy—peak periods and low points—and these vary from person to person. They've also found that scheduling demanding jobs for high-energy times is what makes some people more productive.

Solution: Work with nature rather than against it. If you're not aware of your own cycle, chart it for a week. Then match your more difficult jobs to your peak energy periods—demanding physical jobs, budgetary adjustments, etc.—and save the low ebbs for routine or sedentary jobs—menu planning, sorting laundry and storing it.

Recognizing your particular scheduling problems is the first step toward changing your behavior, but to actually make real and lasting improvements requires action. Concentrate on one problem at a time, because breaking old habits demands effort and persistence. Choose the easiest problems to correct as your first challenge. Once you've gotten those under control, take on the slightly more difficult ones. One delightful side benefit of recognizing some of your time problems is that they will go away almost automatically as soon as you acknowledge them. For example, if you focus on how much you dislike wasting time waiting in bank lines, you'll either decide to bank by mail, or take the time to make notes for yourself in your planning notebook.

The Weekly Time Chart

The only way to get an accurate picture of how you're spending your time is to keep a written record for one week. Keeping such a time log is a demanding job but so valuable in helping you get control of your time and deciding how to use it more productively that it's well worth the exertion. Remember that it's a device to help you and not a punishment. And make it easier by filling it in during the natural breaks in your day. What you want to discover is whether you're taking too long to do low-priority jobs, if you're letting time slip away because you're not clustering jobs that would be done most efficiently all at once (for example, making all your phone calls late in the afternoon after your prime time), if you're shopping for food too often, and so forth. Once you have a dependable record, you'll be able to eliminate duplication of effort, time wasting that you may not be conscious of, and an overly demanding schedule of difficult jobs without any breaks. You'll see whether or not you need to plan more quick-and-easy meals. And you'll be able to find time for activities that you can't make room for now.

Photocopy the chart before you fill it in and add notes about how you felt (stressed, relaxed, etc.) next to each entry. Some people may need more frequent breaks than others when doing demanding work. By listing your feelings you'll become aware of such needs.

If you discover that you are spending too much time preparing meals, you can correct the situation by consulting cookbooks that offer interesting fast recipes and menus. Or you may need to reorganize your kitchen (see Chapter 6, The Good Cook's Kitchen). If you're spending too long at housework, you can divide up chores with other family members and you may also need to learn more efficient methods of housekeeping (see Chapter 5, Preventive Housekeeping). Or you may need to set limits on time spent on chores to have some rest and relaxation. If you want time to write or paint, you may find that getting up a few hours earlier than usual is not as hard as you would imagine, *after* you've already launched your project.

After two or three months of corrective measures, do another week-long time log to see if you have made the kind of progress you intended. If not, review weak spots and make plans to correct them.

WEEKLY TIME CHART
Week of _____

	S	M	T	W	T	F	S
6:30							
7:00							
7:30							
8:00							
8:30							
9:00							
9:30							
10:00							
10:30							
11:00							
11:30							
12 noon							
12:30							
1:00							
1:30							
2:00							
2:30							
3:00							
3:30							
4:00							
4:30							
5:00							
5:30							
6:00							
6:30							
7:00							
7:30							
8:00–12 midnight							

A Monthly Reminder Calendar

The best way to remember what planned activities are for the coming month is to post a calendar with your activities and those of your family in the kitchen or family room to make sure that scout meetings, doctors' appointments, birthdays, parties, music lessons, ball games, and all other such activities are prominently displayed. This not only gives you and other members of your family a chance to review the coming week's plans on Sunday or Monday morning, it also prevents scheduling conflicts and the bickering caused by not knowing one another's plans. Review and update it on the weekends.

Twelve Targets for This Year

Often we get so busy with everyday chores that we put off changes that would make our lives more pleasurable, better organized, and richer. We talk about having friends in for Sunday brunch, but don't do it. We cut out three or four intriguing recipes a week but never try them out. We decide on exactly which size unpainted bookcase will take care of the clutter in the family room, but we don't go out and buy it. To make sure you do the things you want to do, you'll have to add them to your weekly or monthly schedules.

Here again, reasonable expectations are the key to success. I find that if I make up a list of twelve short-term goals for each year, I actually achieve them. Some of the goals you choose may have continuity—losing five pounds, taking a poetry-writing course, becoming a more efficient shopper, learning how to bake bread—so they become a part of your life rather than a onetime activity. Don't let inertia take over; choose a target date to start whatever it is, and stick to it. And if you want to entertain more often, choose a date for a small party (you're more likely to do it if the number of people is manageable), another date to look through books and magazines for menu ideas (with plenty of do-ahead dishes), another for making out the guest list, to call your

Short-Term Goals	Date to be Accomplished

Long-Term Goals	Date to be Accomplished

guests, and so forth. This is especially valuable for anyone who enjoys entertaining but has to cope with a strong streak of perfectionism. Believe me, it works.

Long-Term Goals

Several years ago after a friend of mine went through a highly emotional divorce, she kept getting severe colds and flu every few months. After two years of this, her doctor told her that he thought she was getting sick so often because she was depressed and seemed to have no plans for the future. "People," the doctor told her, "need something to look forward to." Not an unusual observation, perhaps, but one of which many of us need to be reminded. We may all know that goals for the future give us a sense of direction and anticipation, but even so we may do very little in the way of long-term planning. Many people do make financial plans for their future but neglect travel plans, educational goals, hobbies, and other opportunities for widening horizons. Sometimes a dream is just below the level of our awareness and we need to take some time off to give our daydreams and fantasies full play before we can get to know some of our goals.

Staying on Schedule

By using the Planning Notebook and a family calendar your day-to-day problems with scheduling will soon be pretty much under control. But how can you make sure that you're really moving toward your important goals? And what happens if a big change takes place—your youngest child starts school, your husband gets a better and more demanding job, your own job responsibilities increase? To begin with, simply reread this chapter; set aside some quiet time to reexamine your schedule, priorities, and goals; and talk things over with your family. The best way to make sure you handle change as comfortably as possible is to do a Spot-Check Review whenever you find that a change has brought on stress and confusion. To deal with the more subtle changes that evolve in everyone's life, plan to do an Annual Review, perhaps just after New Year's. It won't require nearly as much time as the major overhaul called for the first time around and it will go a long way toward keeping you focused on what really matters to you.

· 3 · | Managing Money Creatively

Getting your finances in order is one of the most satisfying of all forms of organization. The benefits are so many and so obvious. Not only do you gain a sense of ease and assurance day by day, but you can plan intelligently to achieve both short-term and long-term goals. And when you plan you are much more likely to get where you want to go.

If you've always thought that "being good with money" was a talent you had to be born with—and it wasn't in your genes—you'll soon discover that the skills of money management are easy to master when you tackle them one at a time. By breaking the subject up into small, manageable portions, you'll learn what you need to know. And the more you know about your income, outgo, and holdings, the better equipped you'll be to get whatever it is you want most—whether it's a new washer-dryer, a trip to the Greek Islands, or a larger retirement fund. A side benefit is that when you know you're moving toward a cherished goal, it will be a whole lot easier not to indulge momentary cravings.

Breaking Through Barriers

To obtain a really accurate overview of your financial situation and recognize what needs changing, you have to write the facts down on paper. And that can be a major stumbling block for a great many people. Perhaps they're blocked because they have the idea that only accountants can draw up useful financial statements. Or they may simply not know how to take the first step. As for budgets, despite our awareness that some of our most successful friends are operating with the help of a budget, many of us still consider a financial plan an instrument of torture designed to take all the fun out of life. But if my own friends and acquaintances are typical, I would say that it's the people who have well-planned budgets who enjoy life more. They are the ones who seem to have the investment programs, the snazzy cars, and the winter weekends in the Caribbean. So it makes sense to develop a plan we can really live with and grow with. To help you move forward with ease in creating a workable financial program, the Money-Master Action Plan shows how to make a clean break with old unproductive habits and introduces proven tactics for building an efficient system.

Money is a tool for our use. Yet because it is such a powerful force in our lives, we may lose sight of that fact and find that our emotions are ruling our judgment. Things having to do with money come to be viewed with awe and even fear. As a result we get anxious about perfectly ordinary and simple procedures such as balancing our checkbooks, finding out our credit rating, and keeping sensible income-tax records. Happily, the more we learn about the mechanics of money, the less fearful and more relaxed we become. Like the other areas of organization, this one gets more manageable with practice.

Keep It Simple

Often people who have let their money matters slide into confusion react to the situation with alarm and decide that only an elaborate new system will set things to rights. They choose corrective measures that are needlessly and impractically complex, with color-coded filing cards, multi-columned bookkeeping ledgers, and budgetary plans that look about right for IBM. Tempting as such extreme remedies may appear at first glance, they are usually not the answer. For those of us who can get disorganized in the twinkling of an eye, complex organizing systems are a strain. We're much more apt to be comfortable with and stick to a simple, straightforward plan. In fact, most people find that this is true. When I worked in an accountant's office a few years back, I was surprised to learn that the system they used to keep their clients' accounts was an elementary one that anyone could easily adopt for home use. The professionals I worked with made it clear that the best money systems are the simplest, that anybody can get money matters under control, and that most people can accomplish absolute miracles once they have a sensible plan.

Money-Master Action Plan

Finding out where your money is going is the first step toward getting it under control. The Money-Master Action Plan, a simple two-part strategy, gives you that information quickly and systematically. Even if you've been keeping less-than-perfect records and even if you consider yourself hopeless with numbers, this plan will show you how to start fresh by introducing a very practical method for tracking all your money matters and keeping household accounts. With this plan in operation, you can say farewell forever to worries about disconnect notices from the gas and electric companies and bouncing checks. But more than that, you will have a clear-cut understanding of your spending pattern and you will be able to build a positive program for your future.

The Money-Master Bill Holder. This plain but very useful device is the cornerstone of a system that can provide mastery to anyone who uses it on a regular basis. You will need a small durable box to serve as a holder. The one I use is one of those plastic shoe boxes sold in the five-and-ten. Label the box and date the label. Starting from that day, put in the holder all your bills as they arrive. Also put in supermarket tapes, credit-card receipts, bank statements, refunds, paycheck stubs—everything relating to money for that month. (Remember that this is only for *new financial* items. Do not put in any old papers or any nonfinancial papers.)

Keep the holder in a convenient place near the entrance of your house or apartment, so it will be easily accessible when you sort your mail. I keep mine in a desk that's just a few steps from my front door and, because it's so handy, I find that I have no trouble remembering to use it. Also, to make sure you add and subtract speedily and accurately, it's a good idea to keep an inexpensive calculator in the Bill Holder. Because it makes the task of keeping accounts easier and surer, it's an essential tool for anyone who has been resisting neatness in this area. Store the calculator in the holder and you'll always know where it is when you need it.

At this stage in your financial reorganization, the holder is used to gather together the records you will need to fill in the Cash Flow Chart on page 30, but afterward it can become a part of a practical and foolproof bill-paying system.

The Money-Master Notebook. Buy a very small notebook—one that will fit easily into a handbag, pocket, or briefcase. This will be your record keeper for one month's out-of-pocket expenses—everything that is not covered by the records in your holder. If you are married, you and your spouse should both keep these records. List such expenses as transportation (bus or train fares as well as gas purchases), meals and snacks away from home, cleaning and laundry, movies and other entertainment. Also note down taxicabs, cosmetics, over-the-counter or prescription medicines, cigarettes, chewing gum—every single item you buy.

If you find this kind of record keeping tough going, there are several tricks to make it easier. First, if there are daily expenses that never vary—your fare to work, morning coffee, etc.—you can write these in all at once. Another help is to decide on several fixed times each day when you will enter expenses—perhaps at lunchtime and after dinner. And bear in mind that when you're waiting in line to pay in any store, you can jot down the items you're going to buy. Never wait until the end of the day to make your entries or you'll find that you just can't recall where the money went. For those who find keeping track of such items for a whole month beyond them, keep an itemized list for a week and then multiply the totals by 4.3 to get monthly figures. But make sure you choose a typical week. While you obviously get a much more complete picture of your spending habits if you do a full month's record, the essential thing is to get started on keeping records.

The first time you keep day-to-day accounts, you'll probably be amazed to discover your true spending patterns. You'll locate "leaks" of small expenditures that are placing a strain on your resources and not giving you much in the way of a return. You can quickly start plugging those leaks. But for this one-month period, to make sure you have a realistic picture of your buying habits, keep a record of any items you would have bought in the old days. You want a true-to-life account. If you change your behavior as you go along, you'll have a cleaned-up version of how you've been handling money.

Charting Your Course

Take a minute to congratulate yourself for having completed your month of record keeping. Now you are going to consolidate the information collected in the two parts of the Money-Master Plan so that you can fill in the Cash Flow Chart that follows. Producing this chart, which makes your financial status readily accessible, is a giant step toward monetary order. It will give you a clear idea of how you have been distributing your income in the past. Once you can see the facts all laid out in chart form you'll soon recognize the adjustments that make sense if you're going to attain your goals.

Note that the expense side of the chart is ideal for budgetary planning, so if you make twelve photocopies of it *before* you fill it in, you'll have a sheet for each month of the coming year.

To organize the records in both the Bill Holder and the Notebook, make up a rough accounting sheet of your cash-flow information as follows:

1. Take a yellow legal pad and, using the Cash Flow Chart as a guide, write down all the categories listed under Income, Fixed Expenses, and Variable Expenses.
2. Set aside your paycheck stubs and any other items related to income.

3. Sort by category all bills and receipts in the holder. Then go through all department-store, credit-card, and other general bills, making a list of expenditures by category on your scratch sheet. Methodically go through everything in the holder and make sure that you have a record of all outgo. Using your calculator, add up each category.

4. Because utilities, telephone, and a variety of other categories vary so widely from month to month and season to season, you may want to check back through your canceled checks to study the extent of the variation. Wise planning can allow you to cut back from the heaviest expenditures—by using an attic fan instead of air conditioning on some days and nights, by writing notes and letters instead of making so many long-distance calls, and so on.

5. Go through your Money-Master Notebook and add up your out-of-pocket expenses, category by category. It doesn't matter if you put magazines under entertainment or under educational expense, as long as you are consistent and put the same things in the same categories month after month. Using your calculator, do your monthly totals.

6. Make sure you set aside monthly portions of all expenses that you pay as a yearly lump sum or in biannual and quarterly chunks. These will include school tuition, property taxes, estimated income taxes, and various forms of insurance, as well as membership fees for professional organizations and the like.

A Money Plan That Works

Now that you have a Cash Flow Chart, you can study it to determine any changes that need to be made. Pay special attention to the amounts listed as Variable Expenses because those are the categories that lend themselves to trimming. Also, take note of the fact that Savings are considered a Fixed Expense. Experts in the field have found that the best way to guarantee a sound savings program is to make contributions to it invariable. Too often people with a disorganized approach to money neglect regular savings. When you make a firm commitment to a regular pro-

CASH FLOW CHART

INCOME (After taxes)

Salary	——	Income from alimony, child support ——
Fees, bonuses, commissions	——	Other income (income-tax refund, insurance benefits, royalties) ——
Partner's salary	——	
Interest from savings, dividends, etc.	——	
Cash gifts	——	TOTAL INCOME ——

EXPENSES

VARIABLE EXPENSES		FIXED EXPENSES
		(usually set by written agreement)
Food	——	
Car repairs and garage	——	Rent/mortgage ——
Utilities	——	Estimated income tax (if
Telephone	——	due)
Household maintenance	——	Property tax
Clothing and upkeep	——	Insurance (health, life,
Medical/dental (not covered by insurance)	——	auto, homeowner, other) ——
Personal allowances	——	Loan payments ——
Transportation	——	Alimony, child support ——
Personal care (haircuts, cosmetics, etc.)	——	Union or professional dues ——
		School tuition ——
Contributions to church/charity	——	Other ——
Child care	——	
Entertainment	——	TOTAL FIXED EXPENSES ——
Education/self-improvement	——	
Gifts	——	
Other	——	
TOTAL VARIABLE EXPENSES	——	TOTAL EXPENSES (Fixed + Variable) ——

TOTAL INCOME minus
EXPENSES (Fixed
+ Variable)   ——

Amount available for
Investments, Debt
Payment, Additional
Savings   ——

gram—through payroll savings or automatic transfer at your bank—you're on your way to achieving financial stability.

Another benefit to be gained from your chart is that it shows you the monthly cost of those payments that you will actually make once a year, biannually, or quarterly. If you don't allow for these substantial outlays you can find yourself driven to costly borrowing or to disruptive deferment of other expenses.

When you set out to create a workable budget there are a number of factors that have to be taken into account before you sit down and make estimates and fill in work sheets. First you will want to select goals and discuss timetables for attaining them with your partner and children. Then you will want to consider many possible ways of cutting back on your expenses as well as ways of increasing your income. Only then will you be ready to tailor a plan to your special needs.

Finding a Family Fit

Of course, every financial plan is a matter of compromise and balance. Few people can afford to buy everything that strikes their fancy. And considering some of the items we all occasionally get cravings for, this may be a blessing in disguise. Who among us hasn't had the experience of finding that she or he didn't really use that expensive espresso coffeemaker or the top-of-the-line camera with an array of different lenses and filters or the battery-powered miniature space station? When you're planning a budget for a family on a middle-range income, impulse buying of expensive items is especially dangerous. This isn't to suggest that you get so austere that you eliminate all treats and indulgences, but most people find that postponing purchases of luxuries and other nonessentials provides a valuable cooling-off period. Creating the right financial plan takes careful thought, self-restraint, and open communication.

To make sure you plan wisely, you and your partner will find it productive to set aside regular periods of time—perhaps a two-hour session every week or even twice a week if you need a thoroughgoing financial reorganization—to decide on family and individual goals, to create a sensible timetable for achieving them, and to reconcile the differences that will inevitably arise. Because emotions run high in discussions of money—and no two people react to exactly the same stimuli—choose a time when you're both reasonably relaxed. Also, decide in advance what topics you want to discuss, taking no more than two or three topics a session. That way you can fully explore the facts, feelings, and opinions you both have and work your way through to an accord. One subject many couples have trouble with is how to handle bank accounts, so that should probably be on the top of the agenda. An informal survey among couples of different ages suggests that the range of solutions to this often vexing problem is very broad. Some couples have only one checking account (and either one or two checkbooks) and one savings account; others have two checking and two savings accounts; still others have a personal checking account for both the husband and the wife and a separate household checking account that they both contribute to, plus savings accounts for both short-term and long-term goals. People who use credit cards for a great many purchases may have only a household checking account and whatever savings account suits their needs. This is such an individual matter that you might have to experiment a bit before you find just the system that works best for you.

Kids and Money

If you have children who are school age or older you'll probably want to include them in regularly scheduled money forums. (These would be in addition to ones you and your partner share.) Educating children to the realities of financial life is tougher than ever today because they are exposed to so much high-pressure advertising on TV. But it can be done. And most experts agree that a child of seven is ready to understand a simple discussion of the family's relative financial position and its expenses. But they're all quick to point out that unless you're willing to have your actual income broadcast far and wide, it's best not to tell children exact figures.

Without exception the experts recommend starting a regular allowance at about seven as the best way to teach children to handle money. And the consensus is that after a few supervised buying expeditions your children should have the freedom to spend the allowance the way they want to. That's how we learn from our mistakes. The subject on which both parents and experts disagree is whether or not an allowance should be a payment for chores done or an invariable amount regardless of whether or not chores are done. Some people recommend one approach, while others swear by the other. This is really up to you.

A Balancing Act

Once you have studied your monthly cash flow and discussed your goals and timetables with your family, you're ready to redesign your budget to assure that you move steadily toward your aims. You may decide that you want to keep some of your expenditures at pretty much the same level as in the past, while adjusting others downward (perhaps your food budget and entertainment) or upward (perhaps savings, education to increase job skills). To get things into proper balance you'll have to experiment with different estimates for a few months before you find the most appropriate figures.

Begin by finding out how much income you have to spend on variable expenses each month. You can do this by deducting your monthly fixed expenses, including money set aside for savings, from your income. The amount that remains can be allocated to Variable Expenses, or additional savings, if you have enough. But before you can tackle variable expenses, you'll want to decide on the amount you can designate for savings.

Emergency Savings Fund. If you haven't been planning and saving regularly in the past, your first order of business will be to build up an adequate emergency fund, savings generally kept in a passbook savings account (until you have enough for a money-market bank account) to pay for such common emergencies as unexpected medical or dental bills not covered by your insurance, automobile repairs, replacement of household equipment, and to maintain a cushion when you are out of work and between jobs. Deciding on what is the right amount for such a fund can be difficult. You want to have enough to give you a feeling of security and yet you don't want to keep too much in this sort of account when it could be earning more in treasury bills or other higher interest yet safe investments. Some experts recommend three months' take-home pay as the minimum you should have set aside, while others suggest as high as six months' pay. Ultimately it's up to you. If you haven't got such a fund or the amount you have is less than the amount you decide on, then you will want to put aside a certain amount each month (5 percent of your income is the figure most often cited) and build up an emergency fund that suits your requirements. Only after you have that safeguard will you want to consider other forms of saving and investment.

Trimming Your Variable Expenses. After you've chosen the amount to set aside for savings, you can add it to your other fixed expenses and deduct the total from your monthly income. You'll then know what you have to spend on Variable Expenses. It never looks like enough. Confronting this figure always strikes dread into the heart of the budgeter—one reason many of us have shied away from financial planning. However, with the right approach you can quickly overcome this anxiety. Tell yourself there are a lot of other people who are living well on what you have to spend, because it's almost always true. The secret seems to be approaching the balance of your budget as a challenge to be met and conquered rather than as a punishment to be endured. One way to begin is to select a category like food or gifts and find out as much as you can about inexpensive alternatives to your present way of doing things. Take advantage of your local library to explore books on how to save money. Send for government bulletins on ways to reduce expenditures. Investigate one area at a time, choosing whatever suggestions appeal to you most. For now, and for your next month's budget, begin with the ideas listed below:

1. Cut back on food expenses by planning and shopping systematically—using a list, choosing low-cost foods whenever pos-

sible, taking advantage of specials, joining a food co-op, using coupons for foods you buy regularly, buying in quantity at farmer's markets to share with neighbors and friends.

2. Pare down your phone bills. A kitchen telephone in a busy house keeps calls short. If you have teenagers who hang on the phone for hours, establish a maximum time limit for local calls and make them pay for longer calls from their allowance. Make your own long-distance calls at nonpeak hours. Or investigate one of the special low-cost long-distance services. Or write letters and notes instead.

3. Set up a baby-sitting cooperative with friends and swap sitting services to eliminate some of high child-care costs.

4. Review your gift list and start planning your gift choices far enough in advance to take maximum advantage of crafts fairs, swap meets, and your own creativity.

- Dream up thoughtful gift combinations. Why not a cookie cookbook (paperback, of course), a cookie cutter or two, and some exotic spices; a fishing book and some dry flies or other gear; a tennis book and a jazzy visor.

- Make your own gifts in batches. Consult a "gifts from your kitchen" cookbook or country crafts books from your public library. Visit folk-art and crafts shops and gourmet food shops for further inspiration.

- Visit a big up-to-the-minute stationery store or artists' supply store and choose appealing tablets, notepaper, multicolored pens, and other gift items.

5. If you're buying lunches and snacks away from home, start toting homemade goodies. That way you can assure good nutrition and save at the same time. Good for dieting too.

6. Set up a neighborhood paperback-and-magazine exchange. Or pool reading matter with fellow church members or PTA members.

7. Review your cleaning bills to see whether you're overdoing it. Too-frequent cleaning is not only expensive, it's destructive to clothes. And you can do spot cleaning as well as steaming and pressing yourself.

8. Review your Variable Expenses to find other good places to cut down.

Increasing Your Income. If, even after you've made adjustments in your variable expenses, you find that you do not have enough income to meet current expenses or to set aside adequate amounts to achieve your short-term (one- to three-year) goals and long-term (five-year-to-retirement) goals, you will have to find ways to increase your earnings. This may consist of more profitable yet still safe investment of your savings, part-time work, and such activities as baby-sitting and newspaper routes for your kids. There are a lot of interesting ways to make extra money. Consider some of the possibilities below.

▪ Do you have money in a passbook savings account that could be earning more interest in a money-market fund or a certificate of deposit? Read up on money-market funds before you choose the best one for you.

▪ Are you keeping money in your checking account that should be earning interest? Keep only enough in checking accounts to cover current bills.

▪ Part-time sales work—of cosmetics, kitchen wares, vitamins, and health-food products—can be a good source of income for women. You might want to check recent books on sales work for pointers on how to begin and how to proceed.

▪ Catering parties, baking cookies, and cooking gourmet specialties and fancy desserts can all be income-producing activities if you have that skill.

▪ Offer services for busy full-time professionals—gift shopping, organizing a move, organizing a picnic or child's birthday party can lead to a lucrative home-based business.

▪ To find money-making ideas that suit you and your talents, explore a variety of possibilities. Start by talking to women or men you know who are making money in ways that interest you. Ask your friends for their ideas. Then consult books in your local library or attend workshops at the YWCA or adult extension courses on the mechanics of running a home-based business. Once you start researching this area you'll find that intriguing possibilities abound. But arm yourself with knowledge so that you know what it takes to succeed. Start small and build your venture gradually.

Every month as you learn more about money saving and money making, you can review your budget to see if improvements are possible. Are you and your family able to live within the limits you've set? If not, is it because you've cut back too far or is it because unrealistic expectations have crept into your thinking. It's very easy to get caught up in a continual round of wants, so we all have to consult our true priorities to get back on an even keel.

Tracking Your Expenditures

Walking around with a calculator in one hand and a notebook in the other is not my idea of living the good life. But, after you've decided on your budgetary goals for the month, how do you find out whether you're staying on target or overshooting the mark? While you probably want to keep some kind of record of your outgo, you don't want it to blight your life. I've found that a practical answer is a Countdown Sheet on the three or four most important categories of your spending—perhaps food, clothing, entertainment. (You may also want to do this for your credit-card purchases to assure that you keep those at a safe level. More about credit later.)

Here's how a Countdown Sheet works. You write down the category and the amount you've budgeted for it on a sheet in your Money-Master Notebook. Then, every time you make a purchase in that category, you deduct it from the budgeted amount. It's an easy way to keep track—and it alerts you to the need for cutting back if you're overspending as you approach the halfway mark in the month. And the good part about this system is that most people find that they actually do it!

A Foolproof Bill-Paying System

Once you've used the Money-Master Bill Holder as a tool for gathering together one month's records of income and outgo, you will find that you can employ the holder to create an efficient bill-paying system and make your record keeping almost effortless. Always keep only one's month's records in the holder. Time your bill paying so that you do it a day or two after the arrival of your bank statement. After you've balanced your checkbook (directions follow) and you know what's in your account, you can write checks to pay your bills with assurance. If you prefer, you can also pay bills on the day after your payday. Either plan can work, but assigning a regular time to this chore is essential if you want to keep everything shipshape. Keep only unpaid bills, current money records, and your calculator in the holder. Be methodical about transferring paid bills and bank statements to folders for yearly records. You'll need these if you itemize deductions on your income-tax return, and they are useful whenever you want to reassess your budget plans.

Balancing Your Checkbook

I once knew a highly successful writer who confessed to me that for years he didn't know whether he had $5 or $500 in his checking account. He acknowledged that this made writing checks a pretty hazardous business, but it injected a thrill into what would have been a basically ordinary undertaking. After a while, he found that the problems caused by too many bouncing checks outweighed the excitement, so he opted for the serenity of a balanced checkbook. If you too have had one thrill too many from checks that boomeranged, you can develop a simple system for keeping your bank records in order. The procedure to follow is very simple.

1. Always record every check that you write—by filling in the stub *before* you write the check. If you find yourself skipping this chore when you use checkbooks with separate sheets for listing

checks, order end-stub checkbooks, which have a stub for every check, and remember to write the stub first.

2. Balance your checkbook the day your bank statement arrives, or the day after. Give this job top priority on your To Do list when you receive your statement.

3. Go through your canceled checks and put them in numerical order. Compare the checks to the list on the statement. In all the years that I've been doing this I've always found that the checks matched the bank's listing, but I once got somebody else's check, so banks do make mistakes.

4. Compare the checks to the stubs in your checkbook, putting a check mark on the stubs of the returned checks.

5. On the back of your statement or on the envelope you will find a printed form to use in reconciling your records with the bank's. Fill it in with all the outstanding checks (go through your stubs and note all those without check marks). Add these up.

6. Make a list of all deposits (from deposit slips or records on your stubs) and compare them to the bank's list of deposits. Note all deposits made after the closing date of the statement. Add this figure to the closing balance listed on the front of the statement. Deduct the total amount of your outstanding checks from this figure. This should be the balance listed in your checkbook.

7. Remember to make allowances for monthly charges and other debits. Some people deduct the monthly service charge in advance—and it's a good precaution.

8. If there are any discrepancies between your figures and the bank's, review everything to make sure you haven't miscalculated or overlooked something. If you still find an error—more than a couple of dollars—go in to discuss the matter with the bank. Despite computers (or sometimes because of them) there are such things as serious bank errors.

Handling Credit with Care

Using credit to obtain goods and services now and pay for them later is clearly a great convenience. With a credit card we can buy a color TV on sale and enjoy many months of musical specials, movie greats, adventure stories, political programs—all in vibrant color—as we pay off our debt. If the sale price is a good one, we will save money even though we have to pay 1.5 percent interest every month. And our charge cards offer other advantages as well. We can shop without carrying around a lot of cash. We can take advantage of seasonal sales even when we don't have extra cash. We can take a holiday flight to a family reunion and pay off the cost gradually afterward. Also, when we want to exchange or return purchases in a retail store, we generally get a better response if we have charged them.

No question about it, credit gives us a great many benefits. Unfortunately, it also makes impulse buying and binge spending much, much easier. Sometimes we forget that charge-card buying means we are incurring debt. We find ourselves buying clothes, last-minute gifts, household appliances that cost a bit more or even a lot more than we would spend if we were paying cash. We see something we want on a day when we need cheering up and we forget that we're already carrying our maximum debt load. Credit buying can easily become a problem instead of a blessing. The bills do have to be paid. When we put ourselves in a credit crunch, deferring some bills, paying only a small portion of others, the time has come to reassess. We need to look at the way we use credit, and we may need to get professional financial counseling.

Financial experts have found that there are a number of guidelines that can help us use credit wisely. Here are the points they make:

• Do not have a lot of cards. The more you have, the more tempted you will be to use them.

• If you have any doubts about an item, stop and ask yourself whether you would buy it if you had to pay cash.

• Do not make any large purchases without careful consideration and without consultation with your partner.

• Keep a record of credit purchases (see Tracking Your Expenditures on page 37) so that you will not exceed your safe debt level, which for most people is between 10 percent and 15 percent of their take-home pay. Mortgage payments are not included in this reckoning of a safe-debt level.

• Consult consumer buying guides to discover the best inexpensive models of appliances, cameras, equipment, and cars.

• Get acquainted with the various ways to borrow (read current articles and books on this vital subject) and learn the actual cost of the various kinds of loans and forms of credit, so that you can determine the most beneficial loan for you.

Perhaps the best way to sum up all this advice is to say that we should be well informed about our own situations and about the subject of credit and borrowing. Only then can we take full advantage of the various forms of credit.

Protecting Your Credit Rating

The first time I heard about credit ratings and the bureaus that compiled them was several years ago when I was having a serious conversation about my financial future with a friend who was a high-powered businesswoman. I was a little uneasy about the whole idea of a bureau compiling a record of my bill-paying habits, my bank loans, and how I handled my charge accounts. But my friend urged me to get a copy of my report because she felt that everyone should get his or her rating every so often to be well informed and also to make sure there were no mistakes. Seeing my look of alarm at the mention of mistakes, she assured me that it was not difficult to have mistakes corrected.

So I wrote TRW (one of the several thousand credit bureaus across the country) and for a small fee in a couple of weeks I had a copy of my report. It was not the least bit frightening. All it was was a straightforward listing of my charge accounts and the fact that they were paid up, my bank credit card and the amount owing, my current unemployment, and how long I lived at my current address. What it listed was exactly the kind of information you would want to know about a borrower or customer if you were going to make a loan or extend credit.

Since that time I've learned more about the ratings and the bureaus. Many of the bureaus (you can locate those in your area through the yellow pages of your phone book) are connected by means of teletype machines with a central computerized file of past and present credit information that has been supplied by banks, finance companies, retail merchants, credit-card companies, and other creditors. The information that is supplied can be carried only for seven years unless you have declared personal bankruptcy, which can be carried for fourteen years. One reassuring thing that I've learned recently is that if you have a good explanation for what appears to be negative information (lateness in payments or unpaid bills owing to illness, a troubled divorce, or being unexpectedly laid off) you can supply the explanation and the bureau will add it to your file. They will even set up an appointment to tell you how to submit the information. Corrections can also be made by sending in the relevant information. So check your own credit rating to make sure it's in the best possible shape.

Taking Some of the Torment Out of Taxes

Obviously, paying income taxes is never going to be totally torment-free. But you can make it a great deal less painful and get all the benefits you deserve if you keep good records. (To make sure you do this, get a copy of the IRS Publication 552, "Recordkeeping Requirements and a List of Tax Publications," and when you've got that, do read through the List of Tax Publications, which can be tremendously helpful.)

Since you've now organized your money matters, the records you will need to keep for filling out and supporting your return will seem almost a breeze. To make sure you don't overlook anything, get out your tax return from last year and review all the areas in which you made adjustments and deductions and took credits. If you're a salesperson or you work at home, you may find it helpful to buy one of the excellent new paperback tax guides to see if you're taking maximum advantage of the tax laws.

How long do you have to keep your copies of income-tax returns and supporting documents? Normally the IRS has three years to challenge or audit a return (that is, three years from the date the taxes were due or two years from the time the taxes were paid, whichever is later). But if the declared income on a return is 25 percent under the actual income for that year, the IRS has six years to challenge a return. Also, if your income varies greatly from year to year you may want to take advantage of income averaging, which can reduce taxes; and for that you will need five years' tax returns. So it is probably safest for most people to keep six years' returns, and to store them in a fire-resistant metal box for maximum security.

Monitoring Your Money Matters

One good thing about taxes is that to prepare your tax return you have to review your financial situation once a year. Of course, you can pay your taxes and still not be handling your money well. But assembling all the information required to fill out your tax form does give you the opportunity to go one step further and reevaluate your financial situation.

Once you've gone through the suggestions in this chapter point by point, you'll have all the tools you need to put your money matters in order. To keep them that way, you have to monitor yourself from time to time. A big full-fledged review is best done after the first of the year in preparation for tax time. Spot-Check Reviews are in order whenever you find yourself exceeding your budget or when unexpected expenses crop up. And looking on the bright side, you might find that your savings have mounted up sufficiently for you to put some of that money into certificates of deposit (CDs), treasury bills (T-bills) or perhaps to open an individual retirement account (I.R.A.) if you don't have one. Make sure you have a really sound investment guide (there are several good paperback books in this area) so that you'll be able to tend your money and make it grow.

• 4 • | Putting Papers in Order

Although just about everybody agrees that managing time and money are top-priority activities, a surprising number of people don't give much thought to setting up a comprehensive home filing system. Or perhaps it's more accurate to say that we usually think about it only when we find ourselves awash in a sea of clippings, lists, coupons, photos, and personal documents or after we've just spent a number of frustrating hours tracking down an important paper that has gone astray. There's nothing like spending a whole afternoon or evening searching for the warranty for your ailing vacuum cleaner or a treasured recipe for Christmas cookies or an urgently needed vaccination certificate to turn your thoughts to the systematic organization of your papers. But translating thought into action is very easy to postpone.

On the basis of an informal survey, there's evidence that a great many of us make do with a rather hit-or-miss system that often consists of a strongbox, which holds some of our official documents and financial papers, and a couple of cardboard accordion files, perhaps one for appliance warranties and operator's manuals (though why is the one you want never in there?) and another containing a miscellany of recipes, photos, decorating ideas, school report cards, and diet secrets. And chances are that most of us have a significant number of additional papers stuffed into desk and cabinet drawers, packed away in unmarked cartons, and tucked in between the pages of cookbooks, address books, and notebooks. All told, it's hardly what you'd call a systematic approach. Yet no matter how awesome and unruly a collection you've amassed, read on, because help is just around the corner.

To start, it's reassuring to remember that most of us have only two kinds of personal papers to set to rights. There are *essential documents*, such as birth and marriage certificates, passports, wills, deeds, insurance policies, canceled checks, medical records, and the like; and *special-interest papers*, such as personal letters, photos, recipes, children's art and stories, hobby information, travel information, restaurant reviews and recommendations, and similar items. Clearly the methods for handling the two categories aren't going to be the same, and each of them will receive a full discussion of its own. But because a great many people have combined the two groups into one massive conglomeration, it usually helps to use an Instant-Action Step that provides a way to sort through the accumulation and begin to impose some order. Using the following Instant-Action Paper Plan, you'll be able to call a halt to confusion and keep your papers reasonably tidy as you take steps to set up a workable long-term system.

Instant-Action Paper Plan

In getting papers organized, the ultimate solution is a filing system that will allow you to retrieve any paper easily when you want it. You may decide to "file" some papers in a safe-deposit box for security, some in your Money-Master Bill Holder for easy bill paying (see Chapter 3, Managing Money Creatively) and some in A-to-Z accordion folders, or you may actually buy a handsome filing cabinet and stow your records in that. I'll discuss the various alternatives in detail when I present the comprehensive organization of papers. But before you launch the big push, there is a simple procedure that will help to introduce order right now. It's a simple two-part plan for handling all incoming papers (with certain exceptions, which are described) so that you can be confident of day-to-day order and also lay the foundations for dealing with the profusion of papers from the past.

The exceptions cited above are financial papers. Since valuable papers and money matters are often connected, some of the organizing of our financial papers is covered in the Money-Master Action Plan in Chapter 3. That plan was designed to help you handle all bills, as well as each year's tax-related papers, methodically yet quickly. This Paper Plan complements the Money-Master Plan by providing an easy-to-use system for dealing with all your other mail and incoming papers. In both plans you attack a small but obvious problem area. This approach reflects my conviction that starting small is the soundest way to attack any organization problem.

For most people, incoming papers will consist of mail, magazines, and newspapers. If you have children, you'll also have their drawings, paintings, and stories as well as report cards and other records. It seems safe to say that even if you have a large family, the amount of material coming in every day is easily manageable.

The Mail Minder. In a desk or chest of drawers near the main entrance of your home, allocate two drawers for holding your mail. One drawer will be used for the Money-Master Bill Holder, which is described in the preceding chapter. The other will serve as a Mail Minder, files for temporarily storing incoming mail. After you've put all bills in the Bill Holder, review your other mail and throw away everything you don't want. Getting rid of unwanted paper of all kinds as soon as you can has to become a point of honor. Don't let clutter get a toehold. Next, assign the remaining mail to one of three folders: a To-Do File for anything that requires action, Important Papers File for documents that you will want to keep permanently, and Special-Interest Files for such items as catalogs, health-club schedules, and other items of temporary interest.

The To-Do File is where you will put personal letters, invitations, an application for a new driver's license, an announcement for jury duty, a dentist's notice to set up an appointment, and other mail that requires follow-up. If you have time, do whatever is required immediately and transfer any appointments to your calendar or the big family calendar in the kitchen (see Chapter 2, Making the Most of Your Time). If you can't do everything right away, make a note to yourself in your Planning Notebook and deal with this later. If you have not taken care of all items by the weekend, set aside half an hour to finish all your To-Do File activities and to begin setting up First-Step Files for vital documents and special-interest material. If you are serious about getting your papers in reasonable order, the first steps you take have to be assigned an adequate amount of time and they have to be realistic. Biting off more than you can chew can be discouraging, but on the other hand you do have to start nibbling.

First-Step Files. Getting papers under control is similar to taming a group of wild horses. Once you get them into a corral, you can decide what the next stage of management is going to be. So think of these first-step files as corrals for your documents and clippings.

Perhaps you received an updated version of your medical-insurance policy or some other essential paper in the mail this past week. But even if you didn't, take the time now to begin creating a secure, consolidated file of your essential documents. You will probably want to refine the system later and you may even want to transfer some documents to a safe-deposit box. At this time, however, the important move is to assemble and store in one place as many valuable papers as you can lay your hands on. Buy a fire-resistant metal file box and find a convenient place to store it. Ideally, it should have a lock, and you and your partner should both have keys. If it doesn't lock, assign a storage space to it high in a closet near your desk. Collect all the important papers you now have distributed in various drawers, boxes, and chests, sort them into broad general categories, and tuck them into file folders and then into the box.

The other area to begin organizing will be your special-interest materials—clippings, booklets, lists. Buy four or five legal-size accordion files, the kind that look like paper briefcases. Eventually you may want a folder for each separate area of interest or you may want to set up files in a small file cabinet, but at this stage you're just going to round up materials and sort them into broad categories. If you're a confirmed collector, this could be a major undertaking, so do only one big category a week. For example, you might start a file for all food items and mark it Recipes, Diet Ideas, Party Menus, Nutrition. A folder on design and home maintenance might include Decorating Ideas, Storage Suggestions, How-To Projects, and Gardening. Another possibility is a folder of kids' projects. Before you file them, go through the items to see whether you still want them. Also weed out duplicates. Why save three almost identical versions of Salade Niçoise? If the differences intrigue you, simply note them all on one recipe. Even though you are sorting these to make them more accessible later, as you review the projects and recipes you might want to pull out several you'd like to try out in the next few weeks. Look for timesaving, fast-but-fresh ideas, space-saving suggestions, coupons that will save you money. Take advantage of all those useful ideas you've been saving to give an extra boost to your reorganization efforts.

Record Keeping Made Simple

Often when people talk about getting organized, what they mean to a large extent is having an efficient record-keeping system. Knowing exactly where your important papers are can save you time, money, and stress. And if you've ever spent hours tracking down an insurance policy or some vital data about a job you had ten years ago, you'll know just how frustrating and exhausting disorganization can be. Because so many different subject areas are involved, creating a workable system can appear overwhelming. But like most other jobs, if you divide the project into small, manageable portions and set aside regular blocks of time each week until you finish the job, you'll find that getting your papers in order is no big deal. What's more, once you've got things in order, keeping them that way is practically effortless.

Obviously the kinds of important papers you have will reflect your individual experience, but chances are you'll find the major areas you want to include in the checklist below:

- Personal documents
- Insurance policies
- Financial records (credit cards, bank accounts, pension/profit-sharing plans, stocks and bonds)
- Property records (real-estate records, household inventory)
- Medical records
- Employment history
- Motor-vehicle history
- Appliance and equipment records

Choose the ones you want to include in your files and then rank them in the order you'd like to follow in creating them. Next, read the discussion that follows about what you might like to include. If you give this job top priority and get it done quickly, the reward will be a marvelous feeling of efficiency. Keep the files simple but thorough enough to be really useful.

Personal Documents

Birth, marriage, and death certificates are included in this file, as are copies of wills (originals are best kept in a safe-deposit box), passports, separation and divorce decrees, duplicates of Social Security cards, diplomas, citizenship papers, custody agreements.

Insurance Policies

Having your policies all in one place and accessible is essential so that you can make claims promptly and efficiently and so that you can periodically review your coverage to see if it's adequate. In addition to the policies themselves, you might want to type up a fact sheet that will quickly provide you with the significant facts about each policy. On that sheet you might list the name of the insurance company, type and amount of coverage, your agent, the telephone number, amount of deductible, who is covered by the policy, and the amount and due dates of the premiums. For life-insurance policies, you'll want to list the beneficiaries.

Financial Records

Credit Cards. The fastest and easiest way to obtain a record of all the important information about your credit cards is to put them face down on a photocopy machine and snap their pictures. Write phone numbers next to each so that you can quickly report theft or loss.

Bank Accounts. The information, bank statements, and other papers will be kept in your Money-Master and Tax Records holder (see page 26–27).

Pension/Profit-Sharing Plans. Keep all documents and statements having to do with these in your home files for periodic review because some require you to take fairly early action for the best retirement planning.

Stocks and Bonds. The actual certificates are usually held in your broker's or banker's vault whenever possible because replacing lost or stolen stocks and bonds can be quite an ordeal. But keep a record of stock certificate numbers, dividends, gains and losses on stocks, as well as interest rates, maturity dates, and other significant information on bonds on fact sheets in your home file.

Property Records

Real-Estate Records. Deeds, title papers, mortgage documents, tax-assessment papers, records of capital improvements should be included. Because deeds and title papers are difficult to replace, many people keep these documents in their safe-deposit box (see discussion, page 51–52).

Household Inventory. This invaluable record (a detailed list, with photographs when necessary) requires effort but is well worth it in case of theft or fire. Do it one room at a time, listing all your possessions with their date of purchase and original cost when possible. Keep the inventory in your safe-deposit box and the copy in your metal file. A detailed list of appliances and equipment with serial numbers is also a good idea.

Medical Records

Keep a medical history for each family member, listing serious illnesses, injuries, inoculations, surgery, as well as food and medical allergies.

Employment History

In addition to copies of your résumé, make up a list of job information not usually included on résumés—for example, names of your immediate supervisors, starting and ending salaries, and anything else you think might be useful.

Motor-Vehicle History

Most of the information about your car that you will want on file will be included on the registration papers, in the manufacturer's booklet, on repair bills, and in other forms. If you do not have a manufacturer's booklet, which usually contains checklists for noting checkups, tire rotation, major repairs, and other important information, simply keep a small notebook in your glove compartment and begin to record information on your own, then at the end of the year just transfer any crucial information to your files.

Appliance and Equipment Records

When you fill out the application for a warranty on any appliance or piece of equipment, photocopy it so that you have a record of purchase date, where purchased, and other relevant data. If the operating manual does not have the model number on it, write that as well as the serial number directly on the manual. Also, keep repair bills in this file.

Should You Have a Safe-Deposit Box?

Expert opinion on this subject seems to be that anyone who has hard-to-replace papers, such as property deeds, stock and bond certificates, and contracts, would be wise to have a safe-deposit box, which is unquestionably the most secure place to keep valuable documents. Annual fees for boxes are nominal (about $15

for a small box and $25 for a medium-size one). When you obtain
a safe-deposit box at a bank, you will be given a key and a duplicate, but the bank will retain a key that must be used in conjunc-
tion with your key to actually open the box. So a bank employee
will accompany you to the vault to open the box. For safety's sake
you will have to provide identification every time you want access
to the box even though you have the key. It's a good idea to give
the duplicate key to someone you trust so that in an emergency,
if you cannot get to the bank, the other person can go. (You'll
have to give that person's name to the bank.) Keep the key in a
safe, inconspicuous place, perhaps in a small box in your sewing
basket or in your bathroom medicine cabinet. Although most people keep the originals of important documents in the box, they
also keep copies of everything in their home files. Having only one
copy of any important paper is just too risky. Also, your will
should be kept in a safe place such as your lawyer's office, since
your safe-deposit box will be sealed for a legally required length
of time upon your death.

Checklist of What to Keep in a Safe-Deposit Box

- Birth certificates
- Marriage certificates
- Deeds
- Titles to automobiles
- Contracts
- Bonds and stock certificates (sometimes held in broker's
vault)
- Household inventory
- Separation and divorce papers
- Custody papers
- Death certificates
- Adoption papers
- Citizenship papers
- Valuable jewelry

Special-Interest Files

Some people seem born to collect clippings. When I was growing up, there was a rule in my family that no one could cut anything out of a magazine or newspaper until every other member
of the family had had a chance to read it. My mother invented the
rule to defend herself against a tribe of chronic clipping collectors
who snipped every conceivable kind of article, poem, photograph,
and coupon. If you are coping with a similar clan, you may want
to adopt the same rule. It works—if you get family members to
sign off with their initials on the first page.

If collecting printed matter is in your blood, you'll undoubtedly
need more extensive files than noncollectors do. I have friends
who admit to recipe collections in the high hundreds and instructions for enough craft projects to last a good thirty years, so
among my small circle the clipping mania seems to be rampant.
The question any compulsive collector has to confront is: What
do I do to tame the accumulation? It seems safe to assume that
anyone who would file clippings in a well-marked file the
instant they're clipped would probably not be reading this
book. So the system I've devised has a temporary way station
built into it.

Future-Filing Drawers. Use the bottom drawer of a desk or
chest to store clippings as you cut them out. By designating a specific drawer for this purpose you gather all your recent (and not
so recent?) clips in one place. It helps to control the clutter and it
cuts short searches for items. Also, the eventual pileup of material will force you to file the stuff.

Subject Files. Use heavy paper accordion files for these. Be
sure they are clearly marked with categories that suit your collection. Put all decorating ideas together, all recipes together,
and so on. As you store new clippings, review the collection to see
if there are any you'd like to try out soon. Then store the folder in
a deep drawer, in a chest, or on a closet shelf. I like to keep mine
pretty accessible because I like to review them fairly often. If
you'd like to have your papers instantly accessible, you would

probably prefer a file cabinet with standing files. There are brightly painted metal ones and inexpensive unfinished pine ones to choose from.

To-Do File. A paper file folder with inside pockets is handy for this. All stationery stores sell these. If you want to try out some quick weeknight recipes you've been saving or send away for a handsome country basket, or copy a haircut you saw in a magazine, this is the right place to stash them. Use one pocket for personal activities and the other for household activities.

Kitchen Recipe Box (or other Special-Interest Box). This is the place to keep frequently used, time-tested directions—be they recipes, needlework plans, garden information, or anything else you'll use a lot.

Sharing the Secrets of Your System

No matter how logical your filing system may seem to you, it's just possible that it won't strike others the same way. If you've ever tried to unravel the mysteries of an absent friend's filing techniques, you'll know that people can do some pretty unexpected things. But since the real problems you'll encounter will most likely have to do with important documents, you can simply put a list of vital papers and where to find them in the front of your filing cabinet. Such a list is also valuable for keeping track of dead files of tax papers and the like that you may have stashed away in a closet, attic, or garage. It will save everyone a lot of trouble—maybe even you.

Following Up on Your Filing System

Even if you have everything in a well-marked file, you can have problems with the sheer size of your collection of papers. Some people develop a weed-as-they-go method that keeps files manageable and up-to-date. Others find that a couple of Sunday afternoons in winter are well-spent on reviewing files. Start with recipes and you might find a wonderful main dish to brighten a winter meal or a superstar cookie recipe you can bake as you sort through your papers. Whatever works for you is fine, but it is essential to plan some kind of review to keep your papers accessible and under control.

5 · Preventive Housekeeping

Not long ago a newly divorced friend complained to me that he had discovered that life was 90 percent maintenance. He seemed so downcast that I attempted to console him with the comment that once he was back in practice he'd find the whole process a lot easier. But minutes after I left him, it occurred to me that he'd probably never been very adept at the maintenance side of life. A great many people—women and men alike—never do learn the most efficient techniques of home maintenance. In fact, most of us consider the subject unworthy of even a tiny portion of the thought and planning we willingly lavish on jobs, hobbies, and a variety of other pursuits. As a result we end up doing household jobs in a haphazard way, and often with the wrong equipment. Such disinterest can make the whole process a great deal harder and more time-consuming than it has to be.

Yet, at the other extreme, I've found that many of the books and articles on how to cope with housework complicate rather than simplify the proceedings. To my way of thinking they make running a household sound like running a Holiday Inn. Too often the ingenious shortcuts they devise have to do with chores that most busy people don't want to do in the first place. Perhaps these authors are inherently more domestic than I am and actually enjoy polishing copper pots, scrubbing linoleum to remove waxy buildup, and rubbing down marble tabletops with a chamois and tin oxide. But if the joys of housekeeping aren't native to you, it's

probably wisest to avoid all copper utensils, linoleum that requires waxing, and marble tabletops that get lots of wear. That
way you solve problems before they start.

Obviously it's possible to devote almost every moment of every
day to the maintenance side of living—but is that really living? No
matter how much we may want a sparkling and orderly home,
most of us don't want to be dominated by the mechanics of taking
care of things. So to keep home maintenance in its proper place,
I've developed a system called Preventive Housekeeping. First it
shows how to eliminate many jobs completely through careful
planning and then it goes on to facilitate maintenance with a combination of the correct tools and energy-efficient techniques. Putting the system in operation may require an extra expenditure
of time and effort at the beginning, but it very quickly reduces
housework to the civilized essentials. What's more, it's adaptable
to various kinds of households and can easily be tailored to your
special needs and schedule. The secret is to proceed methodically
through the Super Six Housekeeping Rules:

1. Get rid of all unnecessary belongings. Eliminate all unused
equipment and clothing, impractical furniture, temperamental
houseplants, etc.

2. Make sure you have the best storage you can create.

3. Choose easy-care furniture, fabrics, and accessories.

4. Use systematized cleaning methods and professional tools.

5. Set up a practical maintenance schedule for you and your
family.

6. Hire outside help for big jobs—seasonal overhauls, window
washing, painting walls and furniture, garden cleanup—whenever you can afford it.

Once you've put the Super Six rules into practice, you should be
able to keep your whole house neat and shining for just about a
half-hour's effort a day, plus about two or three hours (divided up
among your family) over the weekend. I'll discuss the details of
the system later.

At this point I'd like to put in a few words for the psychological benefits of this approach. By keeping things simple and adopting systematic cleaning methods, it's just possible that you'll find many household tasks enjoyable. I don't mean to suggest that you'll invariably whistle while you work, but rather to point out that there can be a soothing and relaxing rhythm to household jobs if you flow with them.

Another possibility is that you'll discover that even when you're organized you still don't like housekeeping. Any number of women have turned their energies to starting a small business, such as catering, word processing, cosmetic sales in order to pay someone else to do all or most of their housework. If you feel that way, by all means consider money-making pursuits that appeal to you, find out as much as you can about them, and start to work. But since you'll probably only be able to afford part-time help at first, it's still important to know how to do household chores with the minimum outlay of time and effort.

Instant-Action Cleanup

Before you undertake the thorough analysis and reorganization required by the Preventive Housekeeping system, you might want to know about a quick cleanup method that you can put into practice right away. It's a once-over-lightly approach that will get your house presentable superfast. Chances are that at one time or another you've actually used some version of it already. If you have ever had one of those heart-stopping telephone calls that announce the momentary arrival of an important guest just when every room in the house was terminally messy, you've probably done something like this. Under that kind of pressure we perform virtual miracles. But the psychic cost is so great we wouldn't want to have to do it often. Well, the Instant-Action Cleanup offers a way to systematize and cool down that frantic performance. You get the benefits without the tension. What's more, with only minor modifications, this system is ideal for home maintenance.

Carry-Along Cleaning Kit

Your first requirement is a portable cleaning kit. People in the cleaning business use these as a matter of course and wouldn't dream of doing their rounds without one. One seasoned office cleaner I talked with said that without it she'd never finish her work. Here's what you'll need for your kit:

- Vinyl mop bucket or a vinyl caddy designed as a carrier
- All-purpose spray cleaner
- Spray window cleaner for mirrors (remember, always spray the cleaner onto the damp sponge rather than directly on mirrors or the glass covering art or photos so that spray does not damage picture frames or ruin art and photos)
- Furniture-polishing spray (not a wax)
- Cleaning rag
- Dust rag
- Plastic sponge
- Plastic scouring pad (with a sponge encased inside)
- Small child's bucket (to fill half full of warm water)
- Small plastic storage bags for trash
- A kitchen timer

If you live in a house with two floors, make up two of these kits and keep one on each floor. Along with the kit you should also take a broom and dustpan (with a string through the handle for easy carrying on your cleaning rounds). Another thing you'll need (though you don't carry it with you) is a box or basket for every room for collecting objects that don't belong where you find them. Store these boxes in a nearby closet when filled or not in use.

The number of jobs per room that you manage to do and the order you do them in will depend on the size of your house, the amount of help you get from your family, your schedule, and what's important to you. If having the bed made is the vital job in the bedroom—the thing that makes you feel all's right with the world—then naturally that will head your particular list. Whatever is especially important to you is what you do in the five minutes. Some jobs you may be able to relegate to every other morning. Experiment for a week or two to see what works best for you.

The best time to do this cleanup is before you leave for work or, if you stay home, immediately after your family leaves in the morning. Do it right away because it will set the tone of your day. Of course, if you're a night owl, you can do some cleanup chores before you go to bed. And you should create a cooperative housekeeping plan with your mate and children. Make sure there's a sensible deadline by which all daily chores must be done.

Before you set out on your cleaning circuit, put the breakfast dishes in the dishwasher or in a dishpan of soapy water. Then wet and wring out the sponge in your kit, and you're ready to tackle your living room. If you have to pass through your dining room to get to the living room, start there. You should move from room to room consecutively. Allow about five minutes per room, except for your kitchen (and perhaps the bathroom), which will take longer.

Living Room
- Pick up and put away books, magazines, newspapers, and such.
- Transfer foreign objects (toys, games, clothing) to pickup box.
- Stack any glasses or other dishes on a table or desk near the doorway for transporting to kitchen later.
- Straighten furniture, plump cushions, brush off any crumbs, dust, etc.
- Dust if necessary.
- Sweep if necessary.
- Use carpet sweeper on rug.
- Empty ashtrays into plastic bag.

Bedrooms
- Hang up and put away clothes and shoes.
- Make beds (children should make their own beds).

- Put dirty clothes in hamper.
- Straighten up tops of bedside tables and dressers.
- Dust and sweep if necessary.
- Empty ashtrays.

Bathroom
- Air bathroom.
- Clean toilet seat, sink, bathtub, mirror, and faucets.
- Pick up clothes and towels (another chore children can do).
- Straighten towels and bath mat.
- Clean floor if necessary.

Kitchen
- Wash dishes or run dishwasher.
- Wash and scour pans.
- Sponge-clean countertops, work surfaces, stove, and refrigerator door.
- Sweep floor and use floor sponge to clean up spills.
- Put away cooking utensils.
- Scrub-clean sink.
- Empty garbage.

Some days you will run late and not be able to do a complete circuit. When that happens, do the living room, the entrance hall, and any other room a guest might see. Rinse and stack the dishes. It assures peace of mind.

Discovering What Needs Changing

Planning is the key to a low-maintenance home. In this case, as in other areas you want to organize, you have to stand back and look at your situation with new eyes. Most of us get so used to our familiar environment and our customary way of doing things that we don't notice what needs changing. We may look at stacks of books piled on a table or toys and sports equipment jammed into a hall closet and not really see them. We don't notice inconveniently placed furniture; we just walk around it. Habit has dulled us to some of our own needs. We may struggle to cope with disorder when a lighter vacuum cleaner, another record holder, a larger spice rack would make all the difference. To achieve the easy-care home we want, we have to disengage from our usual routine so that we can recognize trouble spots.

Just shaking ourselves free of our old habits can help open our eyes to some of our problems. But an even greater help is to make a point of studying rooms that appeal to us in magazines or in friends' homes. Buy several home-decorating magazines and as you go through them pay special attention to bookshelves, storage units, well-designed desks, chests, and credenzas. Become more aware of furniture arrangements. Study the various ways decorative objects are displayed. Try to ignore the too-perfect order, because if people are really living in those rooms, such a flawless aspect isn't the ordinary state of affairs. Next take note of how your friends have solved different problems. Don't be hesitant about asking for advice. If you have a friend who has an expertly organized kitchen, ask her for some pointers. Generally people love to share this kind of information.

Now focus your attention on your own rooms, each one in turn. Where are the difficulties? Does the black Formica table in the living room show every speck of dust? Try covering it with a runner of Indonesian batik or Mexican cotton or a bright handwoven rag rug. Do you always have piles of magazines on your coffee table? Why not get a large bamboo or rush basket for all those back issues, and at the same time add an appealing note of warmth. Do you have too many pottery jars, bowls of seashells, carved birds, and other decorative objects cluttering up your tables and shelves? Adopt the Japanese idea of displaying one beautiful object at a time. You'll find that you really see and enjoy treasured objects much more when you can focus on one at a time. Do you find that you need additional towel racks or towel rings that your kids can reach, more hooks for your closets, laundry hampers for the kids' rooms? Whatever you discover as you examine your rooms, write it down. Some defects you'll be able to correct right away, others will require planning and budgeting.

Remember that very few of us can attain picture-perfect

homes. The goal of all these effects is to have a reasonable degree of order, a smoothly running household, and the freedom to enjoy life more.

Keeping Your House in Order

Now that you've conducted this general survey of your weak spots, you are ready to undertake the five Preventive Housekeeping steps. Putting this into practice is a major operation, so take it one step at a time and apply that step to one room at a time. Reorganizing all the closets at once or trying to change too much too soon can be overwhelming. Do it in installments.

1. *Get rid of all unnecessary belongings.* Start by cleaning out one or two desk drawers and gradually work your way through the desk. Then tackle the bathroom medicine chest. The linen closet. Be ruthless about getting rid of surplus stuff. The recent flowering of garage sales has been a great incentive for weeding out and selling unwanted items. There's nothing like actually getting money for stuff you no longer want. But if a garage sale seems too ambitious, donate your discards to a thrift shop that supports a cause you believe in. By contributing your castoffs to such a shop, you not only help a worthy cause, you also get a tax deduction.

How do you know what to throw or give away? Sometimes it's very easy. Old Monopoly sets with the pieces missing, the tie-dye kit you've never used, two of your six muffin tins, two of the three pairs of badly worn jeans you're saving to paint in. Other than such obvious examples, the gauge of what is dispensable is whether or not you've used it in the past two years. Most articles of clothing, cooking utensils, and sports equipment—to choose the obvious—that we haven't used in two years, we probably aren't going to use. Also, if something is easy to replace for not much money *and* you haven't used it, it's a good idea to chuck it. If something is especially difficult to replace or it has some special sentimental value to you even though it's not especially useful, you'll probably want to store it in a well-marked box.

2. *Make sure you have adequate storage.* Ample storage is absolutely essential if you're going to have a livable house. Some of the tidiest people in the world—the Shakers and the Japanese—are positive geniuses when it comes to storage. And many of the boxes, bins, racks, and baskets they have created to store things in are as handsome as they are practical. For more details on well-planned storage, see Chapter 7.

3. *Choose easy-care furniture and accessories.* Match your style of decorating to your style of living. If you don't want to expend the energy it takes to keep a formal living room looking good, admit that to yourself. A more relaxed style, such as American Country, is much easier to maintain. A mix of Victorian and modern also works well. But be wary of starkly simple styles such as Italian modern, high tech, and some of the very plain American designs. These demand extraordinary neatness to look good.

Choices of colors and fabrics are also significant. Rugs that are very light or very dark both show dirt quickly; velvet textures show marks and scuffs. Get help from a store decorator when you buy any important items. In recent years many couches and love seats have been upholstered in white, pale cream, peach, and other very light colors, all of which show dirt quickly even though they may have a soil-repellent finish. Look for tweedy, textured fabrics in medium-range colors, because these do not need constant cleaning and will wear well.

Some accessories require a lot of upkeep. One example would be copper kettles or decorative bowls that need continued polishing to look their best. Brass lamps and trivets also tarnish quickly, so if you don't want to be bothered with polishing these, use ceramic-based lamps and wrought-iron or tile trivets. Metal ashtrays are hard to clean, so avoid them. Whenever you add anything new to your home, think of it in terms of upkeep as well as attractiveness. Focus on easy maintenance. For example, use comforters instead of bedspreads on your beds in winter, and bright printed sheets by themselves in summer. Seal your floors with polyurethane so that you never have to wax them. Use stainless-steel tableware and save your silver pieces for parties.

4. *Use professional cleaning methods and tools.* Cleaning and

maintenance crews in large urban buildings have mastered all sorts of tricks of their trade. One is the portable cleaning kit I've already discussed. Another is following a regular pattern in both the order of the rooms cleaned and the order of the jobs performed in each room. To be methodical about room order is simply to decide whether you want to proceed clockwise or counterclockwise and stick to that order. The best way to develop a routine for the actual cleaning is to write down a list of chores—daily, weekly, monthly, seasonal—for each room and post the lists in closets in the rooms they relate to or as close by as possible. I'll discuss this in greater detail in the next section.

Using first-rate equipment and choosing it to suit the jobs you have to do is another sign of a professional. It's much better to have an inexpensive though top-rated electric broom than the most elaborate vacuum cleaner in the world, if you can use the broom with greater ease and with it get up dirt quickly and efficiently. So it isn't expensive or elaborate equipment that necessarily functions best. Consult experts in the field whenever you can. Go to the best paint store and ask what they recommend for cleaning painted surfaces, and read consumer publications that rate products. All this will take a little time but will yield high returns over the years in providing you with tools that function well consistently.

5. *Design a practical maintenance schedule.* Because most of us do not like housework, we don't give it much thought. Writing down a list of chores for each room in the house may strike you as excessive if you've been trying to avoid the whole subject for years. But making such lists produces two wonderful benefits (maybe more, but at least two). The first is that it facilitates and speeds up your tasks. Once you've established a routine, you move with more assurance and you proceed with greater ease. To make the procedure as logical as possible, begin the list with big, basic jobs (making the bed, cleaning the tub, washing the dishes) and list smaller jobs in whatever order feels most comfortable to you. The lists that follow are guidelines and reflect a sequence I find comfortable, but do develop your own, and add whatever you think is necessary. In a household with small children, there's

much more sweeping and mopping than there is in a household with adults only.

Every day, before you start cleaning a room, read through the daily list often enough so that in time the contents and order become second nature to you. On Saturday or whenever you choose to do your weekly chores, do the basic cleaning routine before you shop so that you can check to see if you need cleaning supplies. As you put this housekeeping system into practice, you'll undoubtedly discover jobs you've overlooked (often the really scruffy ones you dislike most, such as cleaning the oven or washing out the garbage can). And when you get your new, better-organized life-style fully under way, you may find that you can do some "daily" jobs every other day or even twice a week.

Dividing the chores can be a sticky problem for couples, roommates, and families. It takes some negotiating and effort, but it is solvable. Sometimes difficulties arise because people don't discuss the possibilities openly enough. Trading off can usually be accomplished if people talk about which jobs they like and which they don't. Years ago when I had three roommates, I took over the cooking because I liked to do it and nobody else did. But I never did the dishes, which I disliked intensely. Kids sometimes like chores you wouldn't expect. One crucial thing in getting children to cooperate is to start when they are young and not insist on perfectionistic standards. (More about children and chores in Chapter 9, How to Organize Children.)

In addition to the daily chores listed in the Instant-Action Cleanup, there are weekly, monthly, and seasonal tasks to be done. But these can vary somewhat from household to household, so it's important that you adjust the lists to suit your own needs.

Living-Room Cleanup List

Weekly
Daily tasks, plus:
Vacuum.
Spray-polish wood and vinyl furniture (wax wood furniture once a month).

Spray-clean soiled doors and areas around light switches.

Water plants (plants that require more than once-a-week watering are for hobbyists and not part of normal streamlined routine).

Dust lamps and lamp shades (vacuum shades if necessary).

Dust windowsills and frames.

Dust picture frames and mirrors.

Vacuum or whisk upholstered furniture.

Monthly

Wax furniture.

Move furniture and vacuum behind it.

Clean venetian blinds.

Spray-clean mirrors and inside of windows.

Dust around books and edges of bookshelves.

Straighten shelves and cabinets.

Seasonally

Wax floors (have this done professionally if possible or hire a local teenager or college student to do it).

Shampoo rug (rent machine for this).

Remove books from bookcases, dust books, sponge off bookshelves.

Clean or wash curtains.

Wash windows outside.

Clean closets and cupboards.

Bedroom Cleanup List

Weekly

Daily tasks, plus:

Change sheets.

Dust furniture.

Dust lamps and lamp shades.

Dust mirrors and pictures.

Dust windowsills and window frames.

Vacuum.

Damp-wipe bottles and other dressertop items.
Spray-clean telephone.
Vacuum upholstered furniture.

Monthly
Spray-clean mirrors and insides of windows.
Vacuum venetian blinds and shades.
Straighten clothes, shoes in closet.
Straighten clothes in drawers.
Turn mattresses.

Seasonal
Vacuum mattresses, innersprings, and bed frames.
Wash windows, inside and out.
Polish floors.
Clean and polish furniture.
Clean upholstered furniture.
Shampoo rugs.
Wash or clean venetian blinds.
Clean curtains.
Clean and reorganize closet, store out-of-season clothes.

Children's Rooms Cleanup List

Daily and Weekly tasks just as for ordinary bedroom, plus:

Weekly
Wash crib.
Wash wooden, plastic, and vinyl toys.

Monthly
Sift and sort toys to discard broken (if unusable and unwanted).
Wash toy box, tables, bins, stools.

Seasonally
Check closets and discard outgrown clothing.
Sort and sift out accumulated clutter.
Review toys and supplies to keep in order (negotiate with children about what to discard).

Bathroom Cleanup List

Weekly
Daily tasks, plus:
Spray-clean mirror, medicine chest, shelves, scale.
Change towels and bath mat.
Shake out or vacuum rug.
Sweep and mop floors.
Scour toilet bowl.
Scrub bathtub, sink, and faucets.
Spray-clean soiled areas of doors and around light switches.
Wash combs and brushes (each family member does his/her own).

Monthly
Scour tiles.
Wash or scrub down shower curtain if necessary.
Wash windows, inside and out.
Sort and sift medicine-cabinet contents.
Wash bathroom rugs.

Seasonal
Clean out and wash medicine cabinet.
Wash curtains or blinds.
Clean and air out clothes hamper.

Kitchen Cleanup List

Weekly
Daily tasks, plus:
Mop and wax floor.
Check contents of refrigerator and throw out any spoiled or
    dried-out foods.
Clean refrigerator top, inside door, and drawers.
Spray-clean stove front, drip pans, and around oven door.
Wash stove knobs and spray-clean around them.
Wipe clean cabinet doors and handles.
Clean all countertop appliances and canisters.

Monthly

Defrost refrigerator, empty contents of freezer, and clean with warm mild detergent solution.

Clean oven with oven cleaner.

Wash cabinets, inside and out.

Wash windows, inside.

Clean hood over stove and exhaust filter.

Clean out toaster or toaster oven.

Seasonal

Remove and clean jars from spice rack, clean rack, and organize spices.

Clean inside of cupboards and replace shelf paper.

Weed out unused utensils.

Clean up flatware and utensil drawers.

Wash windows, inside and out.

Keeping Up Good Houskeeping

After you've developed a system that works for you, you'll find that good-enough housekeeping has become almost second nature. Even so, there are going to be times when the system breaks down because other activities intrude such as the arrival of unexpected visitors or when your son decides to bring home his baseball team. There's no such thing as the perfect system for all occasions. So how do you make adjustments if you feel you're already on overload? One way may be to reassign jobs within the family. Another may be to hire a professional or a capable neighborhood teenager to do a few of the big jobs. Try to maintain a crisis fund for times when you urgently need help, or even when you crave a break from a too-heavy schedule. A small expenditure can give you a mini-vacation and a new sense of enthusiasm when you get back to your routine. Give yourself a break!

•6• | The Good Cook's Kitchen

I f you were to visit a professional cook or even an enthusiastic amateur who does a lot of entertaining, chances are you'd find a kitchen to envy—orderly, efficient, comfortable. It makes sense that as they master their craft, serious cooks just naturally single out the most effective work tools, plan their work areas to make their jobs easier, and organize storage so that what they use most often is closest to hand. By following their lead, any cook can create the same kind of well-organized and personally satisfying kitchen. It takes careful thought, sound planning, and some hard work, but you will reap the benefits every day, day after day. And the best part is that you don't have to figure out the solutions to all those kitchen problems from scratch. What the pros have learned through trial and error, you can discover in short order by devoting a few hours to the work sheets, checklists, and suggestions that follow.

Getting Back to Basics

How can you achieve a kitchen that makes cooking and serving meals easier and more pleasurable? What is the secret of entertaining with a minimum of fuss and frenzy? I think it can all be summed up by "getting back to basics." You have to have the right equipment for the kinds of cooking you do, but not a lot of extras. Your work space has to be designed to accommodate the food you prepare as well as the utensils you'll need. You shouldn't have to hunt for a piece of equipment you use regularly.

The quickest way to identify your particular kitchen dilemmas—if they don't just leap out at you—is to make a systematic study of the five areas people usually have trouble with. This sounds harder than it is, and the effort you do expend will pay off with giant returns. You'll want to consider these areas:

1. equipment
2. storage
3. work centers
4. service and cleanup
5. meal planning

Obviously there will be some overlapping among these areas, but focusing on each separately will help you recognize your special trouble spots.

Instant-Action Kitchen Correctives

Since thinking about changes is a lot easier than actually making them, it's essential not only to recognize your stumbling blocks but to get into action quickly to correct them. This instant-action plan has been designed to lead step by step from planning to corrective measures.

1. Using a big yellow legal pad, write down each of the five areas listed previously, one to a page. Go into your kitchen, settle yourself on a stool or chair, and think about each area as you look around the room and re-create your activities. On each sheet write down whatever comes to mind.

2. Now, read through the section of this chapter that relates to each area, paying special attention to your own known weak spots and then writing possible solutions next to your problems.

3. After you've reviewed all five areas, decide on a quick corrective step for each, something you can do right away to make your life easier. It can be as uncomplicated as transferring wineglasses from the kitchen cabinet to a shelf or tray near your dining area. Or you might clear away all the extraneous stuff from your countertops—store the blender you use only in the dog days of summer, throw away the broken egg timer, give away the jar of hot pepper jelly no one in the family wants to try, stash the tube of instant-mend glue in a handy drawer. Another quick-and-easy step would be to alphabetize your herbs and spices so you don't spend twenty minutes looking for the oregano the next time you make spaghetti sauce. Do one thing in every area so that you get the feeling you're moving forward on all fronts.

4. Finally, make a list of all the remaining corrective steps you want to take. Decide on a sensible but speedy schedule (remember how easy it is to put this kind of thing off indefinitely!) and mark the steps down in your own personal calendar and on a calendar you will hang in the kitchen. And don't forget to break big jobs down into manageable portions. Tackling too much at once can be discouraging and lead to disorganization in other areas. Once a week make it a point to check your calendar to make sure you stay on schedule.

Equipment—the Right Tools

Very few people escape the predicament of equipment overload in today's kitchens. With rare exceptions, people have too many gadgets and utensils. Cooks tend to be irresistibly drawn to kitchen gear, even things they secretly know they have very little use for. And often equipment is kept in the wrong place. It's amazing how quickly we accept the location of something that is inconveniently placed as though it were predestined. Another frequent kitchen affliction is trying to function without some vital piece of equipment—a really good chef's knife, a colander, a timer. Since all of the problems in the equipment area are easy to solve, this is a terrific place to start your kitchen makeover.

The Make-Believe Move

How do you go about weeding out all the unnecessary equipment you've accumulated? Where do you start? I've found the answer to both these questions is quite simply to pretend you're moving. Recently I learned at first hand the cleansing value of moving when I had to move twice in one year. Happily, you don't have to go through the dislocation of a real move. You can enjoy the benefits without the traumas.

There's real hard work involved in this fantasy move, but it's a marvelously freeing experience. And you can proceed at your own pace—as long as you proceed!

Here's what you do:

1. Get three or four cartons from your supermarket or liquor store.
2. Read through the list of Bare Essentials (below) and check off whatever you want to take with you (in your imaginary moving van). Obviously, you should add any of your own special indispensables.
3. Transfer your essentials to one carton, or two if necessary.
4. Any utensils and gadgets you don't think are essential should be put in boxes marked Kitchen—N.E. (nonessential). These will be stored for later consideration.
5. You should now have one or two empty drawers, as well as several empty cabinets.

Sit down near your cartons of indispensables. Before you put anything back, think about where you use each item. Would it be more useful hanging from a hook near the stove, at your work center, next to the sink? Should you keep it with other utensils in a drawer, in a pottery mug on your work area? Strainers are most useful hanging near your sink, rather than stored on a shelf behind several saucepans. Spatulas and pancake turners are always available when you need them if you have them hanging from hooks or horseshoe nails near your stove and not mixed up with other utensils in a drawer.

Don't put things out unless you can put them out in the new place you've decided they belong. This is going to be your new trouble-free kitchen, so no more half-hearted attempts. Make a list of any nails, screws, or hooks you'll need as well as any racks or lumber.

Store boxes of nonessential items in a hall closet for the time being. You may want to retrieve a few items—but do so with great caution. From now on any implement you bring into the kitchen should have a real purpose, or in no time you will duplicate the pileup you had before. Clutter is the enemy of the efficient worker. Stay bare and spare for as long as you can.

The next step in your make-believe move is to evaluate your appliances, glassware, and china. Are you using them enough to keep them in their present locations? If not, where should they be moved? Are you not using some of them at all? If that's the case and you have no sentimental attachment to them, put them in a box for your next garage sale or make a tax-deductible contribution to a thrift shop. Do not keep a whole set or even part of a set of dishes just because Aunt Sally gave them to you. You can keep one cup and saucer if you'd like a memento.

Be just as ruthless about appliances you don't use. Most of these are bulky and space-consuming. Often we have them because somewhere in the back of our minds we believe that a well-equipped kitchen should have a waffle iron, or an electric mixer, or a toaster oven. But if you don't use them more than once or twice a year, maybe you could find a smaller and handier replacement. For example, a hand beater (electric or not) can replace a full-size mixer if you need it mostly for small jobs. Or maybe you can do without the item completely. Another possibility is to replace a very useful electric appliance (electric can opener, electric knife sharpener) with a more compact hand-operated version. Now is the time to take an inventory of everything you have.

Of course, what is an essential piece of equipment for one cook is totally superfluous for another. You'll have to make the decision as you go along. But for now I thought it might be helpful to provide a list of what is generally considered a basic set of tools for the good cook. And once you have your tools properly located, you'll find cooking is easier and much more fun.

Bare Essentials

1 paring knife
1 serrated bread knife
1 10-inch chef's knife
1 carving knife and fork
1 knife sharpener
1 long-handled wooden spoon
1 long-handled slotted metal spoon
1 long-handled basting spoon
1 pancake turner
1 spatula
1 rubber scraper
1 set tongs
1 long-handled two-tined fork
1 set measuring spoons
1 set measuring cups
1 small wire whisk
1 rotary hand beater
1 strainer
1 colander
1 cutting board
1 set ovenproof mixing bowls
1 vegetable peeler
1 small hand grater

1 9-inch square cake pan
1 small saucepan (1½-quart)
1 can opener
1 bottle opener
1 corkscrew
1 potato ricer or food mill
1 funnel
1 9-inch pie plate
1 coffeepot
1 teakettle
1 10-inch frying pan (with cover)
1 7-inch frying pan (with cover)
2 cookie sheets
1 rolling pin
1 roasting rack
1 1-quart casserole (with lid)
1 2-quart casserole (with lid)
1 5-quart casserole (with lid)
1 candy thermometer
1 medium (2-quart) saucepan
1 large (3–4-quart) saucepan
1 muffin tin

Specialty Items

Beyond the basics are the specialty items you'll need for various ethnic cuisines and for baking and dessert making. Read through the questions below as you consider the implements in your kitchen nonessential boxes. Most people do not need a paella pan, but it may be that you use yours for a lot of other things beside paella. Many ethnic tools can do double service. A Chinese cleaver is an outstanding example of this. Ask yourself:

1. Do you cook Chinese food often? French? Italian? Mexican? What equipment makes your foreign favorites much easier to prepare?

2. Do you make bread weekly? Cookies? Other baked goods?

3. Are desserts one of your specialties? Do you need soufflé dishes, custard cups, a Bavarian mold?

4. Do you cook fish and shellfish regularly?

Although you may not need as many specialty items as the cookware store would have you believe, it is smart to have the implements that suit the kind of cooking you do. Steamers and fish poachers might be useless to one cook and invaluable to another. If you love to cook Chinese food you may want a wok, a bamboo-handled strainer, and a cleaver. Of course, you can get by without them. It's a matter of how much space you have, the size of your budget, and how much you enjoy the feel of Chinese utensils. Probably the best rule to follow when you're tempted by any exotic equipment is to buy it cautiously, one piece at a time. Once you get adept at using it, you can add another if you still want to.

Storage

Has anybody *ever* had enough kitchen storage space? Even people with big Victorian kitchens manage to achieve a packed-to-the-rafters look. There seems to be a version of the Peter Principle at work—possessions increase to fill the space available. When we have a pantry or lots of shelves and cabinets, we buy more and larger provisions, stock up on sodas, indulge in wine bargains, and we also save jars, paper bags, and the like. But in most of today's houses and apartments, finding space for really necessary objects is often the challenge. Success in meeting that challenge is the result of a positive attitude and ingenuity. Amazing things can be achieved.

Once you've eliminated, through your imaginary move, all the stuff that didn't belong in your kitchen, the next step is to organize what remains. Assign the most convenient spaces to the objects you use most, slightly less convenient places to second-string equipment, and so on down the line. Be very methodical about this, using the front of easy-to-reach cabinets and shelves for things that have top priority, backs of those same shelves for things you use fairly often, and harder-to-reach shelf space for things you may use once a week or less. Obviously, you can move things around if you misjudge frequency of use, but inertia is a powerful force and once something has been placed on a certain shelf, we have a tendency to let it stay there. Also, you have to decide whether you want things out in the open or put away. There are a number of practical and imaginative ways to keep things easily accessible. You'll find there are whole books on storage, including one or two paperbacks on kitchens. If you have major problems in this area you will find lots of helpful ideas in these, so it would be worth your time to consult them at your public library or to buy one of the paperback editions. Usually these books provide detailed how-to instructions and plans.

For most of us the solutions to our storage difficulties lie in adjustments made to already existing cabinets and shelves, the addition of one or two new ones, and the creative use of racks, hooks, and other hanging storage. The checklist that follows offers a variety of simple solutions to common problems.

Ideas for Increasing Open Shelf Space

• Vinyl-coated stacking shelves on counters add a second layer of space for canisters, recipe file box, teapot. Open-fronted stacking bins also work well on counters as well as inside cabinets.

• Handsome copies of Shaker and Colonial hanging shelves are ideal for spice shelves and small utensils. (Check furniture-kit catalogs.)

• Stacking shelves made from cutting boards mounted on two small boards are easy to construct and offer solid support for blender, processor, juicer.

• L-shaped brackets attached to walls with wall studs can support pine shelves from the lumberyard. Have the boards cut to desired size. Stain, paint, or finish boards with polyurethane.

• High-tech industrial metal shelving units—standing and hanging—are handsome and practical. Along similar lines, a baker's rack provides both counter space and shelving.

• Combine handsome ceramic bricks (or old-fashioned red bricks) with cut-to-measure glass for small shelves on countertops.

• Attach vinyl-coated-wire dish rack to wall to hold plates in upright position.

• Use wooden or bamboo bed trays (the kind with fold-down legs) as stacking shelves on your counters.

• Coated-wire rolling carts can be used to store everyday tableware. (After dishes are washed and dried, simply stack in cart.) Use additional shelves to hold napkins, mugs or cups, and a plastic bin for flatware.

Ideas for Increasing Closed Shelf and Cabinet Space

• Use vinyl-coated-wire stacking shelves inside cabinets to double space for storing canned goods, glasses, custard cups, soufflé dishes, etc. (You can build your own stacking shelves to specification out of inexpensive lumber finished with polyurethane.)

• Freestanding plastic stacking drawers can fit inside floor cabinets or closets or on counters. Add on new shelves as your space and budget allow.

• Stacking baskets of reed or bamboo add a country note as well as useful space to hold kitchen towels, sponges, party equipment, etc.

• Lazy Susans of all kinds can help make the most of cabinets, especially those at floor level.

• Stack one particle-board cube on top of another (paint them a bright cheerful color first) and place these against a wall. Use one, two, or three pairs as space allows and cover top with butcher block or pine boards from the lumberyard.

• Plastic bins or coated-wire bins fit into a rack to make drawers in floor cabinets.

Ideas for Hanging Storage

• Attach strips of lath to wall and add brass cup hooks or other hooks to hold small utensils.

• Shaker peg racks (ready-made or in kits) hold pot holders, kitchen towels, baskets, other gear.

• Colonial-style salt boxes or knife boxes make ideal holders for small utensils, flatware, etc. (Check catalogs for kits, assembled versions, or books with easy how-to directions.)

• Hanging knife racks are easy to make at home and a wide variety of magnetic, ready-made are available.

• A towel bar or two attached to underside of hanging cabinets makes a dandy holder for utensils on S-hooks.

• Curved metal racks with sliding hooks hold heavy frying pans, sauté pans, etc. (Remember to use heavy-duty bolts and fasteners when you attach racks or shelves that will hold heavy pots or other equipment.)

• A small wooden ladder attached to ceiling with heavy-duty bolts and supported by chains holds a variety of pots with S-hooks. (Boat-supply stores have brass S-hooks, and housewares stores offer vinyl-coated ones.)

• Vinyl-coated grids hold small racks, bins, stemware holders, hooks for small utensils, and a variety of other holders. (Add new ones as budget allows.)

• Three-tier hanging wire baskets hold onions, small utensils, cookie cutters, etc.

• Dowel mounted on hooks and supported every few feet holds S-hooks for cooking equipment.

• Two-tiered vinyl-coated-wire rack holds pot lids and paper bags.

Special Note About Hanging Storage: Make a point of combining similar objects on a rack for good looks. Hang all of your enameled iron pots from one rack, and so on.

Cold Comforts—An Organized Refrigerator

If you're a single parent with one child, you're not likely to have too much trouble keeping your refrigerator neat and clean. It may occasionally get out of hand, but it's generally manageable. All you have to do is check through the bins and foil-covered containers once a week to make sure you're not growing penicillin or harboring shriveled carrots and such. But larger families know how terminally messy a refrigerator can get in the twinkling of an eye. They will find that a real system for refrigerator storage goes a long way toward eliminating hassles, confusion, and waste. In the beginning, you may find it necessary to keep a chart of the shelves taped to the refrigerator door. Also, one person should be assigned the job of reviewing the contents at least once a week (probably just before a major shopping expedition) to see what is happening way back on the shelves and in all those plastic wrappings. If you do this regularly, you'll never end up with dried-out cheese, moldy oranges, and unrecognizable fuzzy things.

Work Centers

Look through any recent decorating magazine and you'll see glorious pictures of big country kitchens and big city kitchens that make you forest-green with envy, especially if you're an apartment dweller confined to a kitchen that could double for a closet. But nice as it is to have room enough to work efficiently, the truth is that many large kitchens are remarkably impractical. The stove and sink are usually too far away from each other and the refrigerator a short hike away from the central work space. Also, large rooms can encourage tiring work habits and lead to a glut of useless equipment as well as collections of items that don't belong in a kitchen at all, such as schoolbooks, sports gear, and the like. Obviously, it's not good to work in a tiny cramped room, either; but even a very small kitchen can usually be reorganized to allow smooth functioning. Some of the best cooks in the business practice their art in smaller-than-average kitchens.

The key to an energy-efficient kitchen (the cook's energy, that is) is to have the stove, sink, and refrigerator form a conveniently spaced triangle. You should be able to move quickly from one to another in a few steps or simply by pivoting. Of course, you can't change the size of your kitchen, unless you want to undertake a major remodeling job. But you can make a great many practical and affordable adjustments to create a comfortable, step-saving work center. Often the answer is a well-placed work island or a work table on casters with a butcher-block top. A vinyl-coated-wire rolling cart can be a blessing in both large and small rooms. You can keep it outside the very small kitchen most of the time and use it to transport vegetables and meats to a work area just outside the kitchen if that is necessary. Since you are the one who knows and understands your needs, you will be able to devise the best solutions.

The primary work center in large kitchens—and often the only one in small rooms—is the food preparation center. It's an area within easy reach of the stove and sink. Often it's a portion of the counter that's been equipped with a cutting board and that has easy access to herbs and spices and knives and other implements. For convenience in a small kitchen this can be a butcher-block shelf that is raised and lowered between uses or a board-topped cart. It is absolutely essential that you plan this area to suit your personal requirements. For the next few weeks pay attention to how often you have to search for a piece of equipment or how often you have to cross the room for some utensil. Make sure you move everything you use frequently to nearby storage spaces.

In large kitchens many people like to have a secondary work center for baking, a place for mixing and kneading bread, for mixing and rolling out cookies, and for other baking activities. This keeps the primary center free of confusion and mess and allows two cooks to work at once. Also, you can cluster ingredients and equipment you use only for baking near this area. When you plan either work center, think of yourself as candidate for a cooking teacher's program on TV. By thinking of yourself as a professional, you'll find yourself naturally planning for maximum performance on a daily basis.

Service and Cleanup

If the thought of having guests for a meal sends shudders of anxiety down your spine, it probably means that you need to spend some time planning serving aids. Stacking dishes on the open oven door is not the answer. To get at the root of your problems, ask yourself these questions:

1. Can you move tableware closer to your dining area? Most people keep too many of their table utensils and glasses in the kitchen rather than near their dining table.

2. Why not get yourself a serving cart? Being able to cart dishes as well as garnishes, salads, and desserts makes a big difference in maintaining an orderly delivery system.

3. Why not transfer your bar to a convenient spot in your living room? It's a lot easier to bring a pitcher of water, a few lemons and limes, and an ice bucket to the bar than it is to combine bartending with your cooking chores. If you're married or live with a roommate, make a plan beforehand about who will do what. If you live alone, ask one of your guests to take over the drink making.

4. If you have a very small kitchen, why not put a table just outside the kitchen to act as a serving table? When you have ample space to set out serving platters, condiments, and wine bottles, you'll wonder why you didn't do this years ago.

Clean As You Go

Being organized about cleanup is not a magical talent some people are born with and others lack. Like every other kind of organization, it's a matter of planning. And it starts earlier than most people think. Watch one of those TV chefs or a great cooking teacher and you'll notice that they clean up after each step in preparing a menu. If you do the same, you will have a much more manageable job when the meal is over. Here again the rolling cart can be a step-saver and organizer.

Menu Planning

No doubt about it, meal planning once a week makes kitchen organization a whole lot easier. When you plan menus in advance you'll pay attention to what you have on hand in cupboards, refrigerator, and freezer. That not only eliminates waste, it also reduces those maddening extra trips to the market for one or two forgotten items. And you can stay within your budget more easily. Planning provides another advantage by allowing you to balance your work load. You can combine simple and complicated dishes, top-of-the-stove and oven specialties, make-ahead and last-minute recipes. You can cook main courses ahead for very busy nights, wash and dry salad makings in large batches, and make the best use of leftovers. (See Chapter 8 on Shrewd Shopping for a more detailed account of menu planning and shopping strategies.)

It used to be that housewives had a standard series of recipes for the week—for example, chicken on Sunday, meat loaf on Tuesday, spaghetti on Thursday, fish on Friday. The wonderful diversity that today's cooks present to their families is a fairly recent trend. And while variety makes mealtimes more interesting, it's easy to overdo. Do try appealing new quick-and-easy recipes, but save elaborate and time-consuming dishes for weekends. It's often true that kids and even some adults prefer simple, quick-to-make recipes.

When you approach your meal planning, think of yourself as running a very small restaurant. You want to provide good food at a reasonable cost to yourself and with the minimum of effort.

Kitchen Safety

Obviously, you will want to take all the precautions you can when you and your family work in the kitchen, making sure you have enough sturdy pot holders to lift hot pots and pans, allowing food to cool before you taste it, turning the handles of saucepans inward so that they don't extend over the edge of the stove, using sharp knives, blenders, and processors with care. But no matter how careful you are, small accidents are bound to happen occasionally in every kitchen, so minor cuts and burns have to be dealt with. It's a good idea to have a small first aid kit that you keep in a prominent place in your kitchen. You should include plastic strip bandages, peroxide, and spray pain killer. To extinguish small kitchen fires have baking soda or salt easily accessible. Many people also like to purchase a fire extinguisher for more serious fires.

Keeping Your Kitchen Uncluttered

Putting everything in its place is one thing, keeping it there is something else entirely. That's especially true if there are several cooks in the same kitchen. Your own personal situation will dictate how often you should review your kitchen to make sure it's in good working order. It might be as often as once a month, though many people find that once a season is enough. Whatever else you do, make a comprehensive survey of your kitchen in the fall before the holidays. Holiday cooking and entertaining will go much more smoothly if you have the right equipment in the right place, the surfaces cleared for action, and your appliances in top condition.

• 7 • | Stretching Storage Space

No question about it, adequate and convenient storage space is a basic requirement for good housekeeping. But it's even more than that. There is something intensely satisfying about having our belongings orderly and neat. A well-ordered linen closet, a trim and tidy pantry, well-arranged bookshelves, all have a kind of beauty to them. Yet because many people today live in less-than-spacious apartments and houses, they have to plan very carefully or in no time their possessions have overrun the living space. Sometimes the solution is to provide new and better-designed storage, sometimes it's to reduce our collection of possessions, and perhaps most often it's a mixture of both.

To get in the right frame of mind to tackle the storage challenges you're confronting, it might help to think of going on a long sea voyage on a beautiful yacht or sailboat. You have to take everything you value and stash it away so that it's accessible and orderly. And of course you'll want it to look good. This fantasy can start you thinking about priorities and about how people with even less space than you have would deal (and have dealt) with getting things shipshape. You'll want to focus on both the winnowing-out process and the right kind and quantity of shelves, cabinets, chests, and closets to house your treasured possessions.

Now that you have the appropriate mind-set, the next step is to get down to your own very concrete situation. With the best will in the world, all of us collect new belongings and, since we're not really going to be at sea, will continue to do so. Staying on top of such a constantly changing situation requires a system that you can use to get things in shape and then to keep them that way. And that's precisely what the Two-Step Storage Strategy has been designed to do.

Step 1 involves a room-by-room appraisal to decide which corrective measures are required. This will pave the way for Instant-Action steps that quickly remedy the most glaring minor problems. Step 2 resembles packing for a voyage: it calls for cartons and an in-depth reorganization of all storage space to create an easy-maintenance system that will keep you on track over the long haul.

Step-1 Storage—Getting Started

To launch your storage review, choose the room, closet, or cabinet that has been giving you the greatest distress—the one you stare at and mutter, "I'll never get that organized." Get out a notebook and pencil, study the situation, and ask yourself these questions:

1. Are the right items stored here? Should some be moved to another location?
2. How can this space be made more useful? Adding hooks? Towel bars? Bins? Dividers? Half shelves?
3. Do I need to increase the actual storage space by adding a new shelf, chest, basket, hamper?
4. What can I do right now to eliminate obvious clutter and messiness?

Let's choose a few concrete examples. Maybe you've straightened out two desk drawers to get your bill-paying and mail-handling systems in order—but the desktop is still a catchall for magazines, schoolbooks, newspapers, gloves and mittens, and broken crayons or pencils. What's more, the two bottom drawers are so stuffed with knitting, envelopes full of photos, and obsolete bus schedules that they're now nonfunctional. Or maybe the floor of your clothes closet is a confused mass of shoes, boots, and slippers. Or maybe the front entryway of your house is so jumbled you've taken to squinting as you rush by it so you'll miss the grungy details.

Step-1 Storage is a tool for looking at any one of these trouble spots, pinpointing the problems, and getting it all down on paper. On one side of your notebook page, write out a list of the problems and on the other list all the things you think are necessary to remedy them. Go all out: include every corrective measure you can think of to make the space useful and beautiful. Put a star next to those procedures you can do immediately or in the next few days. Transfer these to your To Do list. If you draw a blank when you confront any problem area, seek out books and magazines that might provide solutions. Ask friends (neat ones, naturally) how they handled a similar situation. As you explore, you'll find that there are many ingenious ways to solve any problem you're grappling with.

To organize your desktop you might want to use a group of small baskets to hold supplies and paper, a mug or ceramic jar to hold pens and pencils, and a nested set of small boxes for stamps, paper clips, and staples. The overstuffed clipping drawers call for a Step-2 approach. Most clothes closets can use a good deal of re-organizing, and many of the necessary adjustments are on a Step-2 level. But you can do something right now about the closet floor by cleaning it out, polishing the floor, and restoring just those shoes that you still wear in neat pairs. If you have too many shoes to fit on the floor, buy a shoe rack that hooks on the closet door or a vinyl-coated half shelf to increase your space. Baskets for magazines and books are much more economical than most racks and carriers and usually much better looking, but if you'd prefer, there are angled racks that can hold quite an array, or you might like to make a magazine holder from a sturdy, extra-large cereal box covered with Con-Tact paper. If you can't think of a good solution for some of your problems, make a note to drop by your local library to check out books with storage ideas. Also, check department stores, closet-supply stores, and mail-order catalogs for aids to organizing.

Sometimes a problem has become so much a part of our lives that we have come to accept it as inevitable. But once you've identified the problem and have started looking at it as one you mean to solve, you're on the road toward correcting it. To help that disorderly entryway, you might begin by buying a hanging basket to hold mittens and gloves, a small wooden box to set on a hallway table for papers and magazines (to be emptied once a week), a pottery bowl for keys and coins, and a strip of Shaker pegs for guest coats and umbrellas. If your children's schoolbooks tend to pile up here, you might want to make a rule prohibiting this, or you could add a heavy square basket under the hall table to hold them. Sometimes you'll want to take a firm stand, and sometimes it makes sense to go with the flow.

Whatever your storage problems are, once you focus on them, you'll find yourself suddenly noticing solutions—as you read magazines, look over the model rooms in department stores, and become alert to similar situations in your friends' homes.

Remember that the goal of this initial step is to achieve surface order as quickly as you can and to make you aware of the more serious, deeper difficulties. After you've finished Step 1, your apartment or house will be much more orderly and comfortable and you'll probably feel inspired to tackle the Step-2 projects that will make living even more convenient and trouble-free.

Step-2 Storage—Desk Drawers and Cabinets

Get out your notebook and review what you've written about your current storage needs. Generally the biggest trouble spots are closets, cabinets, and desks. But no matter where you decide to begin, before you can actually start your reorganizing chores, you'll need to collect three sturdy cartons (four if you have school-age children) from your local liquor store. These should be the size that are usually used for shipping wine and they should be made of heavy cardboard. Cut out crescent-shaped handles on the sides, or you can make cord handles by punching two holes in two opposing sides near the top, pulling heavy cord through and knotting it on the inside. Handles will make these easy to lift, and that's important.

You may want to paint the cartons or cover them with washable paper because they are going to become permanent storage tools. One will be used in the living room or family room as a pickup box for gathering all items that do not belong there. Another can be left in the hall closet or near the back door as a temporary deposit box for sports gear, toys, and clothing. The other two are for sorting through your belongings in your Step-2 chores. Mark one Keep and the other Reject.

You may want to attack the bulging drawers in your desk or a chest of drawers in your bedroom. Whatever you decide, the basic procedure is the same. Allow a half hour to an hour for each session.

1. Choose one drawer or one shelf. Sort through all items and distribute into either the Keep or Reject boxes. Later, for throwaways, you'll need a large heavy-duty garbage bag.

2. Don't try to decide where you're ultimately going to put what you keep or how you're going to dispose of the rejects. Just sort through everything in the drawer.

3. After you've finished sorting, if you still have time, put the Reject carton in a closet and, using the desktop, evaluate the contents of your Keep carton in terms of the files you set up in Chapter 4, Putting Papers in Order.

4. Decide what use you will make of the drawer. If it is going to house untested recipes and loose photographs, or any other similar categories, you'll want to get a plastic sweater box for the recipes, a folder and album for the photographs, an accordion file for any other category. For recipes or any other category you want to consult regularly, a box is much more convenient than an accordion file, since it's easier to open and close. You can simply

sort through it on the day you plan your menus. And, when you see that you keep passing over some recipes you've saved, you can weed them out.

5. At another session review the Reject pile. Items from a desk drawer are likely to be such things as train schedules, unmatched mittens and gloves, matches, old greeting cards, and the like. Most will be items you throw away but every so often you'll find something that is a good prospect for your next garage sale.

Step-2 Storage—Hall Closets and Linen Closets

One of the main decisions to make about most closets is what you want to store in them. Too often the value of storage space is lost because people try to stow too many different things in an unsorted mass. One way around this is to mark closet shelves and to store things in marked boxes and bins. Also, it's a good idea to have a bin or basket for miscellaneous items on the bottom shelf of all closets for when you're in a hurry. You can redistribute these to more appropriate places later. This idea is especially valuable for hall closets, which tend to become badly confused easily.

Linen closets are generally the least troublesome of all storage spaces because what to put in them is so obvious. That doesn't mean they can't get disorganized, but just that they tend to be pretty easy to care for. You'll probably have a shelf for towels, washcloths, and mats, a shelf for bed linens, a shelf for bathroom supplies. And if you have space, perhaps a dirty-clothes hamper. For safety's sake you might want to keep dangerous laundry supplies or medicines on the top shelf of this closet out of the reach of children. Review your own Step-1 analysis to see what makes sense for you.

Unlike linen closets, hall closets can turn into complete chaos in a matter of weeks because we put such a variety of things in them and so often. These seem to tempt us to stash things on a temporary basis—which soon becomes permanent. As a result, they require at least twice yearly overhauls. Try the box-on-the-bottom-shelf for temporary parking and see if that keeps the worst of the chaos in check. But to get back to anything resembling a tidy state, you'll undoubtedly have to go through the step-by-step procedure described below. Once again, allow a half hour to an hour for each session.

1. Decide whether you need closet aids: more hooks for the back of the door, some placed so that children can hang up their own coats; more hooks in other parts of the closet for extra umbrellas, a flashlight, the unisex rain slicker (with a name tag in it) that you lend to guests; a row of Shaker pegs to hang hats, caps, and mufflers; a half shelf for boots, etc. Look through catalogs or department-store closet sections for new ideas. Make a list of whatever you decide in your Planning Notebook.

2. Get out Keep and Reject cartons and start sorting through the items in the closet, one shelf at a time. If you find such items as a Monopoly set or a deck of cards, make sure they're complete before you store them somewhere else. Hall closets attract disabled or broken objects.

3. When everything is removed, vacuum the shelf, lay new shelf paper and think about whether a stack of bins or wire drawers or a half shelf would be valuable in this location.

4. Review the coats, jackets, and sweaters you find hanging up. Look for anonymous, discarded garments. Sometimes a guest will leave an article of clothing or a beat-up umbrella and we'll keep it for five years hoping whoever left it will call and ask for it back. If you have such items and they're not useful, you might as well give them to the Salvation Army or the thrift shop.

5. Now check the floor of your closet. Are there always bottles, shopping bags, broken sports gear, overshoes, and the like on the floor? Maybe you need stacking bins to keep such things in order. And just for fun you might decide to paint the floor a bright Chinese blue or fern green or stencil white flowers on a blue background.

6. Before you put back anything from the Keep box, decide how you want to allocate the space. *Mark* the shelves with labels to impress the purpose on you and other family members. Also,

put out-of-use seasonal equipment in marked boxes on high shelves.

7. Once you've marked out the best way to use various shelves and you've eliminated clutter, you can consider adding a thing or two that would make your life easier. Do you often have to change light bulbs here and out on the porch? Maybe a box of bulbs and a small two-step ladder would be a valuable addition. Keep things simple, but also practical.

Step-2 Storage—Clothes Closet

Every now and then a national magazine will do a feature on famous stars' closets. Recently there was one in which the closets were so large that a couple of them were larger than my bedroom. And one of the stars had at least fifty pairs of shoes. As I considered the challenges involved in organizing closets and clothing collections of that magnitude, my own difficulties paled to insignificance. It may sound like sour grapes, but I've convinced myself I'm happier not having to choose from among that many shoes. Anyway, even if your wardrobe is moderate in size, you can still confront some pretty tough issues when you're organizing a clothes closet, especially if you have to share it. For that reason, you'll probably find that this particular chore takes much longer to complete than any of the other storage projects because there are so many different ways you can handle what you store and how.

1. Use your bed to sort the clothes you plan to keep and return to the closet. The Reject box is used as usual, and the Keep box will serve for clothes you can't bear to part with even though you haven't worn them in a while. (I'm cautious about overexuberant cleanups because I once threw away a jeans skirt, decided to retrieve it an hour later, and wore it quite happily for another two years.) Store these "Undecideds" in a small carton, with a list on the side or top. Review them in a quieter moment. Maybe you'll find a good use for these when you have time to think.

2. Stash discards in a shopping bag for easy removal. If you haven't worn something in two years, if you feel depressed when you have it on, if it doesn't fit right and makes you uncomfortable, if the color does terrible things to your complexion—add it to the discard pile. Unless you can see an easy and really workable way to recycle it, don't get stubborn about salvaging something. I've heard of several cases where people ended up putting more energy, time, and money into recycling a mistake than they spent to buy it in the first place. So be as unbiased and direct as you can. Better to let someone else enjoy it than to waste valuable time and money.

3. Before you return clothes to the closet, decide what organizers will help *and which you're likely to use*. I once had a shoe rack that I used only once or twice and then felt guilty about for a month before I finally gave it away. Be realistic—if tucking things into little cubbyholes has never been one of your strengths, it would be better to use a vinyl-covered-wire half shelf or a two-shelf bookcase for your shoes. You may feel that only a drastic and costly renovation would solve your clothes-closet problems when taking the time to arrange your clothes, using organizers that suit your needs, adding bins and boxes to store small items, and painting or tiling the floor can transform your present closet into just what you need.

4. If you need space for sweaters, scarves, and sweatshirts, consider using one or more of those white wire stackable drawer units. They fit easily on a shelf or on the floor of the closet under short clothing such as blouses and jackets.

Continue your half-hour (or hour) sessions until the closet is in tiptop shape. Remember, now that you're aware of the joys of organized closets, stay alert to possible useful additions when you're shopping, reading magazines, or checking through catalogs.

Shelves and Other Open Storage

Some cultures and groups of people seem gifted when it comes to turning a requirement into an asset. This was particularly true of the Shakers, a communal religious sect that flourished in New England and parts of the Midwest during the eighteenth and nineteenth centuries. They believed in utter simplicity in their home furnishings because they thought that ornamentation was sinful. Despite those limitations, or really because of them, they created some of the most useful, beautiful, and practical forms of storage ever devised. So perfectly adapted to function were the things they designed—the racks, boxes, shelves, and pieces of furniture—that most of their storage ideas are just as useful today as they were when they were developed. Beautifully proportioned hanging shelves accommodated jars or boxes of kitchen herbs, books and small personal effects. Freestanding floor racks of pine were used for drying herbs, towels, or clothing. Oak gathering baskets held eggs, garden produce, and balls of yarn. And strips of hand-turned maple pegs adorned the walls of almost every room for hanging clothes, candle sconces, utensils, dried herbs, and even chairs. Not only are high-quality reproductions of their creations still available, but many modern high-tech storage designs are based on their ideas.

When you think about using open storage—bookcases, cupboards, shelves, racks—it inspires you to collect and display decorative objects along with books and records, herbs and spices, coats and scarves. And often you can use open storage to serve a double purpose. You might use a two-shelf bookcase for storing books and records, cover it with flat cushions, and place it under a window as a window seat. Or you might use a handsome small bench for your TV and for several houseplants.

Create your own shelving. Brackets hold a single shelf in the bathroom or kitchen, or you can use one above the other. If you like the flexibility of boards and bricks but you've always felt the bricks had an unfinished look, consider buying ceramic bricks in interesting colors. Heavy glass shelves supported with bricks make an interesting desktop variation. For out-of-the-way storage in very small apartments or crowded homes, consider suspending a hollow-core door on pulleys from the ceiling to hold blankets, baskets of out-of-season clothing, and boxes of Christmas-tree ornaments.

Finally, old-fashioned coatracks are often available at auctions, and these can be interesting additions to any room's decor.

Baskets, Boxes, and Bins

Many people have a kind of mania for baskets—I am among them—and they buy baskets first and find a use for them later. Basket uses seem virtually endless. Small ones in the bathroom can hold guest soaps, manicure supplies, hair implements; in the bedroom, they can hold frequently worn jewelry, brushes and combs, and potpourri; in the entryway, they are ideal for keys and change, mittens and gloves, reminders to other family members, theater tickets. Use them any way you like.

Large open baskets are just right for magazines, firewood, balls of yarn, games in boxes, sports equipment, stuffed animals. And the closed variety has hundreds of uses.

Storage boxes are another of my weaknesses. I have two on the desk I'm working on right now—a small cherry document box that holds schedules of classes, letters to be answered, and ads for things I want to order; and a pine dower chest that holds all the research materials for whatever book I'm working on. My motto could well be, Buy Boxes. Every kind—wooden, plastic, metal— can be useful. I have a rose-covered metal box for holding herb tea on my kitchen counter as well as an ivory plastic one for tested recipes. Without boxes, organization would be a whole lot harder.

Buy unpainted chests and boxes and stain or paint and stencil them yourself. Stack chests painted in complementary colors one on top of the other to make a bedside table. Many people think of chests only as toy boxes or for storing blankets. You can use them as coffee tables or window seats, and store anything you like in them.

Bins are ideal for holding cleaning supplies under the sink in bathrooms and kitchens, but they're also great for maintaining order in other rooms, inside closets and out. Use bins to hold children's mittens, scarves, caps. Vinyl-coated stacking bins are great for scarves and other accessories in your clothes closet. And they're also ideal for holding a variety of hobby supplies.

Solving the Out-of-Sight, Out-of-Mind Problems

While it makes sense to pack infrequently used or seasonal items on high shelves, in storage rooms, or in an attic or basement, do remember to label or mark storage boxes with large lettering *and*—this is important—keep a note in your Planning Notebook or household files about where you've put them. So if you've packed away duplicate custard cups, extra wineglasses, or a hedge trimmer, you'll know where they are when you need them. It always comes as a shock to discover such items years after you stored them, usually when you're moving.

A Systematic Storage Survey

Well-organized closets and other storage spaces are such a blessing that you'll want to make sure things stay that way. Even if you yourself are on guard and have pledges of neatness from family members, and you have house rules about distribution of space, you must continue to be vigilant about disorder and accumulations of things. Unless you are compulsively neat (which is unlikely, since you're reading this book), you'll want to give just enough attention to your storage situation to keep it under control, but not so much that you use up any extra valuable time. Usually that means a biannual survey—in the spring and the fall when you pack away the winter and summer clothes. Many people add a post-holiday review to their spring and fall cleanups. This is such an individual matter, you'll have to experiment a bit to see what works best for you and your family.

·8· | Shrewd Shopping

When people say they love to shop, what they usually mean is that they enjoy those exhilarating jaunts in search of the perfect pair of shoes, a smashing new coat, or a beautiful decorative object for their house. Or they might possibly mean that they get a kick out of diverting trips to garage sales and thrift shops to unearth hidden treasures. But what they almost certainly *don't* mean is that they like those routine treks we all have to make to the supermarket and discount store to stock up on food and other household supplies. For most of us, ordinary shopping is more likely to be debilitating than scintillating. And it's the kind we do most often. Yet the fact is that the minute you approach stocking your household as a challenge and get systematic about it, you'll find that you save so much time, money, and effort that you've added a note of zest to the undertaking. One thing for sure, when you organize your shopping you eliminate more than one source of annoyance and stress from your life.

Since by now you've already organized many important areas of your life—especially time, money, and your kitchen—you'll find that you've laid much of the groundwork for planning your shopping. You know how much you have to spend for food and supplies, what makes sense in terms of scheduling your shopping trips, and you have a bit more experience with menu planning and choosing the right tools for your kitchen. With all those facts at your fingertips, the mechanics of organizing shopping become almost a breeze.

While supermarket shopping is the big constant in our lives, there are other forms of shopping that greatly benefit from an organized approach. There's finding the best buys in home appliances, coping with Christmas shopping and other gift buying, and just generally getting the best buys in linens, equipment, and home furnishings. Although clothes buying can take a big bite out of any budget, it is such an individual matter and varies so much from region to region and life-style to life-style that this chapter is going to focus only on buying household food and supplies, appliances and gifts. Getting these everyday areas under control is essential to living the well-organized life.

Instant-Action Shopping

To give you a preview of how relaxed and efficient you feel when you do regular planned shopping—and save you money right away—the Instant-Action Step for this chapter is designed to get you quickly into organized food buying.

Here's all you have to do:

- Read the section on Supermarket Savvy, below.
- Photocopy the Perennial Shopping List, below.
- Read the midweek ads from two nearby supermarkets and choose the one with the best specials and prices.
- Check off items you'll need on your shopping list.
- Clip any coupons from the midweek ad or from other sources for items you buy regularly; pin or staple to shopping list.
- When you shop take your list and the amount in cash you've budgeted for food (remember Managing Money Creatively?); also take your handy pocket calculator.

This first venture into the world of shrewd shopping will introduce you to the pleasures of being organized in the supermarket, although it's an instant version of what all shopping should be.

Supermarket Savvy

Advance Menu Planning. The first step in efficient food shopping is planning your meals in advance. You might want to start with one week's worth of menus, or even two. To cut down on time spent with cookbooks and recipes, some people like to map out two weeks of meals at a time but actually shop for food week by week. That might work for you, but it does make it harder to take advantage of weekly specials. You'll have to decide which makes sense for your situation.

Advance menu planning offers so many rewards that after you've done it for a while, you'll never consider going back to the old haphazard approach. Knowing what you're going to serve not only makes your shopping more sensible, it makes your work in the kitchen more productive. You can do any number of preparatory steps all at once in advance—washing salad greens in batches, precooking chicken for casseroles and salads, shredding cheese and chopping parsley, and so forth. And you eliminate the frustration and annoyance of trying to put together interesting meals from foods you just happen to have on hand.

Once you've decided what's ahead for the week you'll have a feeling of assurance and you'll free yourself for the rest of the week from worrying about meals. What's more, since you know you have the ingredients you need, you'll stop committing the cardinal sin of nonplanners: buying duplicates and triplicates of specialty items such as spices and seasonings. Anyone who has ever sheepishly added one more jar of taco sauce to an already bulging collection or one more box of poultry seasoning (which you use in about three recipes a year) to the two on the shelf will know how easily unplanned shopping can erode your confidence and your budget.

Another benefit of planning is that it allows you to introduce interesting variety into your meals. You can start using all those recipes you clipped. What's more, you can build in better nutritional balance and greater economy by using appealing low-meat or nonmeat main courses.

One frequently heard argument against meal planning is that

it's hard to know in advance what you'll feel like eating a week later. How can you be sure you'll want chili next Wednesday? Well, the kind of planning recommended here is not so rigid that it doesn't allow for some switching of meals or parts of meals. But, generally speaking, if you choose foods you and your family enjoy, you won't have too many problems with scheduling.

Choosing the Right Market. To find the right supermarket for you, you have actually to visit two or three, even four nearby markets to compare:

- prices
- the quality of meat and produce
- variety and quality of breads, dairy products, and canned goods
- the way they maintain their frozen-foods department

All these factors make a difference, so you should shop in a different store each week and check all of them out.

Begin your comparison shopping by cutting out the midweek ads of all the stores to review the specials offered, the general prices, and the coupons offered. Next, you should photocopy the Perennial Food Shopping List and the Perennial Household Supplies Shopping List and choose ten items on it that you buy regularly. Keep a record of those prices in all the shops you shop in. Pay attention to all the other factors on your tour of the store. Once you've evaluated all the stores, choose the one that suits you best and make that your shopping headquarters. You might get tempted by specials at another store, but, over the long haul, this one-step approach seems to work best.

There are two possible exceptions to the one-step shopping rule. Both can mean substantial savings. First, if you buy beer, soda, and mineral waters in quantity, it will probably be cheaper if you buy these by the case from a distributor and either pick them up once every two weeks or every month or have them delivered. Investigate such services in your area. The other exception might be a discount store for nonfood items such as paper towels, laundry detergents, household cleansers, light bulbs, and the like. Prices on these items frequently are considerably lower at discount stores than at supermarkets. If that's the case, you can make a once-a-month trip there for all your nonfood supplies.

The Perennial Shopping List. Beyond planning, the primary way to get your shopping organized is to create a dependable perennial shopping list—a basic index of all the items you buy over and over again. It may take you several weeks to produce a list that exactly suits your needs. Starting with the sample list that follows will make the process easier, but you'll have to adapt it to your special requirements. You'll find this an invaluable tool. It's easy enough to keep track of foods like milk and bread that you know you buy every week. A list comes in handy for supplies you don't use so often or that you'd like to keep a reserve inventory of. Life is pleasanter when you don't have to rush out to get last-minute supplies every other day.

To keep your household well stocked and running smoothly, all you have to do is keep an Early Warning Shopping List on your kitchen wall or cabinet to make sure you and other family members note down supplies that are getting low. Remind everyone that the list is called Early Warning because you want to know items that have to be bought *a short time before* they run out rather than *after*.

Perennial Food Shopping List

Baked Goods

    Breads:

    Rolls:

    English muffins:

    Crackers:

    Cookies:

    Other desserts:

Cereals and Other Dry Foods

    Cold cereal:

    Hot cereal:

    Flour:

    Pasta:

Rice:

Beans:

Nuts:

Meat and Poultry

    Meat:

    Poultry:

    Canned meats:

    Cold cuts:

Seafood

    Fish:

    Shellfish:

    Canned seafood:

Milk and Dairy Products
    Fresh milk (skim, etc.):
    Dried milk:
    Yogurt:
    Sweet cream:
    Sour cream:
    Cottage cheese:
    Other cheeses:
    Eggs:
    Butter:
    Margarine:
Vegetables
    Fresh:
    Frozen:
    Canned:
    Juices:
Fruits
    Fresh:
    Frozen:
    Canned:
    Dried:
    Juices:
Beverages
    Coffee:
    Tea:
    Cocoa:
    Soft drinks:
    Mixers:

Condiments, Flavorings,
Dressings
    Ketchup:
    Mustard:
    Mayonnaise:
    Salad dressing:
    Vinegar:
    Relish:
    Salt:
    Herbs:
    Spices:
    Other seasonings:
Oils and Shortening
    Olive oil:
    Vegetable oil:
    Other:
Sweeteners, Toppings, Spreads
    Sugar:
    Honey:
    Syrup:
    Jellies and jams:
    Peanut butter:
Soups
Baby Foods and Supplies
Pet Foods and Supplies

Perennial Household-Supplies Shopping List

Soaps and Detergents
    Bar soap:
    Laundry detergent:
    Dishwashing liquid:
    Dishwasher powder:
    Bleach:

    Fabric softener:
    Spray starch:
    Other:
Paper Products
    Paper napkins:
    Paper towels:

Tissues:

Toilet tissue:

Cleansers and Polishes

Cleansing powders:

Spray cleansers:

Ammonia:

Toilet-bowl cleanser:

Drain cleaner:

Metal polish:

Furniture wax:

Floor wax:

Sponges, Steel Wool, etc.

Sponges:

Steel wool:

Brushes:

Wraps

Aluminum foil:

Plastic wrap:

Plastic garbage bags:

Freezer bags:

Freezer wrap:

Waxed paper:

Vacuum-cleaner bags:

Light Bulbs, etc.

Light bulbs:

Batteries:

Fuses:

Food Cooperatives and Farmers' Markets

When I lived in California several years ago I had a number of friends who belonged to excellent food cooperatives. And if a co-operative had been within easy distance of my apartment, I'm sure I would have joined. The fruits, vegetables, and grain products were of high quality and much cheaper than the similar items at my supermarket. Lower prices at the co-op result from the fact that members contribute a number of hours of work each week to provide the services of employees at supermarkets. My friends all felt that the work was minimal and different enough from their ordinary work to be rather pleasant. Also, they enjoyed the people they met at the co-op. So if the idea of joining a food cooperative appeals to you, check the yellow pages of your local phone book to see whether there are any near you. Or check the books in your library on how to start your own.

The best-tasting corn, tomatoes, lettuces, and other vegetables are often found at farmers' markets and farm stands, but the produce sold at these outlets is not usually that much cheaper than the same foods in supermarkets—unless you buy in quantity. But buying from these sources will give you the advantage of unusual freshness, which will probably mean less spoilage and waste. And if you can find nearby friends or neighbors to share your purchases and you do buy whole bushels of peaches and sacks of potatoes, you'll have real savings as well as great taste.

Cashing in on Coupons

One clear-cut benefit of planning your weekly menus and doing up your shopping list after consulting the midweek supermarket ads in the newspaper is that it allows you to build your meals around low-cost specials and seasonal foods. Another, not-so-obvious reward of such planning is the opportunity to use the cash-off store coupons and money-back offers that appear in those same ads. In fact, coupons are so easy to use when you follow this procedure that you'll probably find yourself clipping them and stapling them to your perennial list as a natural part of being organized.

And once you've gotten started reaping the savings that coupons offer, you'll most likely want to branch out and start using coupons from other sources, such as in-store promotions, magazine and mail campaigns. Studies have shown that it's quite easy for the average family to save close to $600 a year by the shrewd use of cash-off coupons (these are the kind you use as immediate deductions at the checkout counter). While money-back offers can also save you a lot of money, they usually involve sending labels and boxtops back to the manufacturer, which clearly takes time and effort. Some people make refunding almost a hobby, but if you're struggling with organizational problems, the time may not be right for such a pursuit now.

However, the only requirements for cashing in on the cash-off kind of coupon is the willingness to collect and sort them and to experiment with different product brands. If you're a steadfast user of one favorite brand of laundry detergent, pet food, or high-fiber cereal, you can't gain the same savings that you will if you're a bit more adventurous. Still, even if you use coupons only for selected items on your list, you'll save an appreciable amount over time—as long as you stick with practical items you would have bought anyway. It's no economy if you get a discount on a high-priced product that you can easily do without.

Keeping Coupons in Order

Collecting coupons makes sense only if you go about it methodically from the start. So don't cut out a single coupon until you've decided where you're going to file them. A drawerful of unsorted coupons might have figured in your old life-style, but it's definitely prohibited in your new, well-ordered existence. The best coupon holders are either an accordion file or labeled envelopes that have been stapled together at one end. To make up categories that suit your own needs, simply consult the newspaper ads and your Perennial Shopping Lists and invent appropriate headings (for example, laundry products, pet needs, baking ingredients, household cleaners). Since most coupons have expiration dates, remember to file them so that those you should use first are on the top of the pile. Simply store your collection wherever you store your Perennial Shopping Lists and use the two together. Once you're well launched into coupon clipping, the whole procedure will be very simple and quietly satisfying.

Buying Household Appliances

Since most appliances last from ten to twenty years, it's clearly worth the time it takes to get all the information you'll need to buy the best. And remember that the best is not necessarily the most expensive, top-of-the-line model. Sometimes the most expensive models are worth the extra expense, and sometimes they have many features that are more decorative than useful. Also, the model for you is one that suits your particular needs, is well made, and is in a price range that fits your budget. If you have wall-to-wall carpets you'll need a more powerful vacuum cleaner than if you have bare floors and a few braided rugs. But even though you know you need a heavy-duty machine, that doesn't mean you should automatically buy the most expensive you see. You'll want to know which of the machines available will perform best, be easy to use, and require the fewest repairs. Usually it's obvious when we need a piece of equipment, but sometimes we think we need something that in fact we could easily live without. I do not have a full-scale electric mixer because I find that a blender and a small hand mixer perform admirably to fill my requirements. So before you do research on the right model, take the time to assess whether you need the equipment at all.

Often we're attracted to appliances because our friends have them or because we've read some glowing report about their usefulness in a newspaper or magazine. Yet useful as the item may be to others, it actually may not suit our life-style or personal interests. A good example of an appliance that can be a blessing to one person and totally unnecessary for another is a food processor. If you cook a lot or cooking is a special interest of yours, these machines can be miracle workers. But if you cook very simple dishes or you cook just as little as you can get by with, a processor is probably superfluous. If you think you may be in the middle somewhere and you're tempted to buy one, why not borrow one from a friend for a week or two to see if you'll use it. Another appliance that can be a mistake for many people is a top-of-the-line sewing machine. These can cost over $1,000 and can be a boon if you sew a great deal, if you make all sorts of complicated garments, or if you consider sewing your hobby. If you sew very little or don't know how to use a sewing machine, it's probably wisest to start off with the cheapest good one you can find. Or take a sewing course at your local Y or adult-education center before you buy a machine. That way you'll be familiar with what a machine does and you'll know whether the extra features are necessary for you. That will also give you the opportunity to discover whether or not you have a flair for sewing and you'll want a fairly substantial machine. You may find that making an occasional skirt or blouse is about as far as your interest goes. You'll be equipped to make a much more satisfactory choice, and you can use the free lessons often offered with machines to polish skills and create something wonderful.

Deciding What Brand and Model to Buy. Once you've decided that you do want a particular appliance and you think that a new one is the best for your long-term requirements, begin the search by looking in store catalogs, comparing and clipping ads from your local newspapers, checking with friends, and then making one or two visits to specialty stores in your area that feature the item you want.

Take a notebook with you on your store visits and write down brands you like, model numbers, prices, and anything else you think may be useful for your final decision making. Begin to narrow down your choices by taking all factors into consideration:

- What are the basic functions of the appliance and does this model perform them well?
- What about the value of extra features on higher-priced models? Are they really valuable to you?
- How much space will this model take up and can you accommodate it in the space you have available?
- Will it be easy to use?
- How much will it cost to run and maintain it?

When you're checking out all the features mentioned above, look for labels and stickers that give valuable information about the quality of the appliance and how much it will cost to run. The ones to look for are:

- Underwriters Laboratory (UL) label or tag, which provides assurance that an electrical appliance meets approved safety standards.
- The American Gas Association (AGA) Laboratories' blue star, which indicates that a gas appliance meets required safety standards.
- EnergyGuide labels, which are attached to all large appliances manufactured after mid-May 1980 and which state how much energy in dollar amounts the appliance uses annually under normal conditions according to tests approved by the federal Department of Energy. These black-and-yellow labels provide in-

formation based on rates of 5¢ per kilowatt hour for electricity, so if you live in an area where the charges are higher than that be sure to make an adjustment.

Another thing you'll want to check is the warranty or guarantee to see what the manufacturer provides under it. And it's important to find out whether or not repair service is readily available. Finally, you'll find it invaluable to check the ratings of various models in the *Consumer Reports Buying Guide*, which you can consult in your local library.

Deciding Where to Buy

Many factors will play a part in your decision about where to buy your appliance after you've decided just which model and brand you want. Obviously, price is a major element. But if you buy your appliance at a discount center, you will probably have to pay for installation, delivery, and perhaps even for having the old model carted away. A specialty store often includes those services in the price. Sometimes you end up saving so little by buying at the discount store—and you lose the value of the specialty store's service department—that it's better to pay a slightly higher price.

Check the yellow pages for discount appliance stores in your area and find out as much as you can by phone about their price and installation or delivery fees for the model you want. I bought my telephone answering machine from a discount store in New York City and paid almost $70 less than I would have in my neighborhood specialty store. And the discount store was very helpful about directions for installing. That kind of saving can make all the difference about whether you can afford an appliance or not. As a general rule it's a good idea to stick with well-established stores that have an incentive for providing a good price and dependable service.

If you're buying small appliances that will have no installation requirements—electric typewriters, irons, blenders—you often get the best price if you buy by mail. Investigate the big mail-order catalogs now available in bookstores to make sure you're dealing with a reputable company or buy by mail from one of the big chains such as Sears, Montgomery Ward, or J.C. Penney. (More about mail-order buying in the section that follows.)

Mail-Order Shopping

Although Americans have been shopping by mail for decades, in recent years mail-order buying has become a passion with many shoppers—and with good reason, because if you shop intelligently by this means you will pay from 15 percent to 30 percent below the usual retail price (sometimes even more). In other cases you may buy by mail to get unique top-quality products—furniture kits that are exact copies of museum originals and sporting goods or camping gear that are durable and dependable. Here again, it's usually best to stick with well-established firms, but if you're in doubt about a store, simply check in the reference section of your public library or in one of the well-researched paperback books on the subject. What are some of the things you should know to make mail-order buying a happy experience?

The Catalog. Begin with an up-to-date catalog so that you know the correct price and so you don't order discontinued items. If the price of a catalog is under a dollar, tape coins to a piece of cardboard. If it is over a dollar, send a money order because a personal check can take up to two weeks to clear.

How to Order. Give all the information required—page number, style number, size, color, quantities—to assure that you get the item you want. Specify whether you want UPS or Parcel Post delivery if that information is relevant; check the catalog shipping table to make the right decision about this. Finally, pay by money order or certified check (if that's required) rather than by personal check because the company will delay shipment until your check clears. Many companies will accept bank charge cards or such regular credit cards as American Express and Diners Club, but you'll have to check the catalog or price list to obtain this information.

What If Something Goes Wrong? Most companies allow a thirty-day period for return of merchandise if you are not satisfied. However, some few companies have a no-returns policy, so be sure that you know the returns policy of the company you're dealing with before you order. Sometimes when merchandise is delivered damaged, the fault is with the carrier and your dealings will have to be with them. However, if the problem is defective merchandise, misrepresentation, or nondelivery, you'll have to deal with the mail-order company. The law is that firms must send ordered merchandise within thirty days or notify you that there will be a delay so that you can cancel the order if you want to and ask for a refund. If you have any of these problems and cannot get satisfaction from the company you're dealing with, you should write to the Chief Postal Inspector, giving a brief account of your difficulty and providing the name and address of the offending company. Because it can withhold mail delivery to the company in question, the Postal Service is usually successful in straightening out difficulties. Write to the following address:

Chief Postal Inspector
U.S. Postal Service
Washington, D.C. 20260

Controlling Your Inventory

Armed with your Perennial Shopping Lists and a systematic approach to stocking your household, you should find shopping an area of life that stays well organized with relatively little effort. Still, most people do find that there are seasonal differences that have to be taken into account. For example, if your kids go away to camp for a good part of the summer, you'll have to adjust the quantities of most items that you buy. Holiday times also require modifications in your buying patterns. By using the personalized shopping list that is adjusted for any entertaining you want to do, you'll be sure to have the basic supplies you need. But holidays usually mean more dropping-by and spontaneous get-togethers, so extra supplies are in order. You'll probably find yourself really looking forward to holidays now that you have this important area under control.

◆ 9 ◆ How to Organize Children

Ask the average mother whether it's possible to get children organized, and the usual response is a laugh and a comment along the lines of, "Whew! It's a *constant* struggle!" But if you visit a Montessori nursery school you'll see children as young as three who automatically put playthings and dishes back where they belong after using them. How do those schools do it? And what about parents who seem to have pretty neat, fairly well-organized children without resorting to continual threats, violent wrangles, and shouting matches? What's the secret of teaching organizational skills to children? Well, actually, the secret isn't a secret. What is involved in teaching children these skills is exactly what is involved in teaching an adult, with a few significant differences. Most adults know that learning is a step-by-step process. So if they miss a step when you're instructing them in something, they tend to ask you to repeat it. With kids you're the one who has to recognize what the steps are, when they should be repeated, and how long the teaching sessions should be. And, of course, you have to have realistic expectations. All children backslide on the road to neatness and other organizational skills.

FAMILY CHORE SCHEDULE

	M	T	W	T	F	S	S
MOM	Lunches Dinner	Dinner	Breakfast Dinner Dishes	Breakfast Dishes Dinner	Lunches Laundry	Kitchen Cleanup Wax Furniture	Dinner
DAD	Morning Cleanup Dinner Dishes	Breakfast Evening Pickup	Trash Dinner	Bathroom Cleanup	Trash Dinner Dishes	Yard	Change Bed
TOM	Breakfast Dishes Garbage	Lunches Dinner Dishes	Breakfast Garbage	Breakfast Dishes Evening Pickup	Morning Pickup Dinner	Vacuum	Brunch
ALLIE	Laundry Evening Cleanup	Breakfast Dishes Kitchen Cleanup	Lunches Evening Pickup	Breakfast Dinner Dishes	Breakfast Trash	Dinner	Brunch Dishes

Instant-Action Step—Talking Things Over

Whether the situation you and your family are now confronting is mild disorder or wild chaos, the best place to start is a family council. Even if you're a single mother with one child, the family council format can work for you. It's a structured meeting that allows everyone to have a say. And that is the beginning of getting a smooth-functioning household again. Use the first meeting to discuss the need for cooperative housekeeping, to divide up chores, to establish a chore schedule, to discuss house rules. Also, talk about the need for learning organizational skills for accomplishing anything from building a model airplane to writing a paper for school to baking cookies. Weekly meetings will reinforce the message that you're serious about the chores getting done, but will also allow all the family to discuss changes that might be needed in job assignments. It's usually a help to write out an agenda of family-council meetings in advance and post the list on the family bulletin board in the kitchen. Obviously, the age of your children and the degree of the problems you face will affect what you talk about at your particular first meeting, but even though parents ultimately have the control, such meetings can be very productive in gaining family cooperation. The first meeting with your family will be the Instant-Action Step in organizing your children, so make sure that you have a concrete new plan and everybody understands what the new work schedule will be before you adjourn. We'll come back to work schedules and co-operative housekeeping later in the chapter, but for now let's discuss planning a child's room for maximum neatness, comfort, and efficiency.

Children's Rooms

All the experts agree that helping children to get organized begins with the right choice of furniture and storage units for their rooms. Furniture should be arranged so that what a child wants to do is easy and comfortable. In addition, children should have step-by-step training sessions on how to perform simple maintenance chores. Because young children are naturally active and like to master new tasks, if parents plan the right environment and methodically go through the steps of putting toys away, simple cleaning and straightening, and bed making, children can gradually learn to maintain their own rooms. But you have to start with simple jobs and you have to have patience.

The Right Furniture. In an effort to avoid too-cute furniture, the kind that's adorned with rosebuds and cherubs, many people go to the other extreme and buy plain, handsome furniture that is unfortunately too large for a small child to cope with. According to early-childhood specialists, small children *need* small furniture if they are to function well and achieve order. Experience has shown that when children have a pleasing, child-size environment, they are productive and orderly; when they are overwhelmed by large heavy objects they cannot move or use properly, they become frustrated and disruptive. Imagine how you would feel surrounded by giant chairs and chests and you'll see how important it is to get your young child small, lightweight chairs, a bed that is small enough to be cozy and makeable, low shelves for storage, and a chest with drawers (perhaps plastic stacking drawers) that a child can open and close on his own.

What is true of furniture is also true of storage shelves, bins and boxes, hooks and pegs. Perhaps because most children have lots of toys and many of them tend to be bulky, we automatically think in terms of large toy chests and bins for holding toys. But small or medium-sized lightweight boxes and bins are best—stacking bins of different colors are great to hold crafts materials, art projects, and construction paper. For small objects—beads, jacks, marbles, and the like, use small containers of different colors—a nest of easily opened boxes in the colors of the spectrum would be ideal—because a child can easily lift, handle, and identify them and this will encourage her to use them for storage. If you say, "Put all the marbles in the green box, all the beads in the yellow box, and the crayons in the red one," you're more likely to get results than if you simply say to a child, "Let's clean up and put everything away."

Remember that shelves should be low and easily reachable—a two-shelf bookcase from an unpainted-furniture store is just right. You might paint the outside one color and each of the interior shelves two other colors so that you use the different colors to assign places to different objects. You can even cut out small pictures of the objects stored to act as guides for where they belong on the shelves.

Hooks for jackets, caps, and mufflers might each be a different color and should be conveniently low so that your child will be encouraged to use them. Consider a strip of Shaker pegs for this purpose.

Finally, artwork, photos, charts that list chores, and certificates of merit with gold stars should all be hung low enough for a child to look at them with ease.

The Right System for Restoring Order. Once you have a room that's geared to the size and abilities of preschoolers, you're ready to teach grooming and cleanup chores. These should be kept to a few easy-to-manage jobs that can serve as the foundation for later, more complex chores. Begin with simple cleanup chores at age three and move on to basic grooming skills—washing face, brushing teeth, brushing hair, and getting dressed. You can devise a chart with pictures that can be photocopied or a permanent chart with pegs that can be inserted when a job is done. Room-cleaning jobs will involve making the bed, which will be a cooperative venture of parent and child at first (and do make it easier by using a fitted bottom sheet and a quilt), dusting with a bright cloth, putting clothes and toys away, and sweeping with a small broom. When you oversee training sessions, remember to use words of encouragement and to applaud small improvements in techniques. After a time the ritual of morning chores will soon be automatic.

As children reach school age you'll want to teach them some of the basic household chores in addition to room maintenance. Setting the table, bathroom cleanup, and straightening up the living room are logical beginnings in this area. Assigning one household job to a child for a whole week seems to work better than other possible arrangements. Whenever you make an assignment, make sure your children know precisely what it is you expect—what the job consists of and when you want it performed. Clear-cut assignments—writing them out is often the answer—are accepted more willingly than general directives to help out.

Reducing the Work Load

Setting up rules of procedure for kitchen and living room, as well as for the entryway and hall closets, can help to reduce the amount of work that has to be done. This is another example of preventive housekeeping. One good example would be to assign everybody in the family a different-colored mug to use for drinks, or a mug-and-plate set for all snacks. These are to be carried to the kitchen and washed by the owner. Using a cleanup bucket (sponge and soapy water) for spills can catch messes before they dry out and become a big cleaning job. Eating and drinking certain foods only in certain places is another possible precaution. No food or drinks in bedrooms might be one such rule. Start a contest in your family and give an award for the best preventive house-keeping ideas. Some suggestions may be a bit on the wild side but others will quickly become household traditions.

Many children are so logical that they startle their parents. A number of children I know have suggested going to sleep fully clothed to avoid the rush and hassle of getting dressed in the morning. Others have carried this idea the whole way and have slept on the floor with their pillow, fully dressed, to eliminate making the bed as well as morning dressing.

Coping with Collections and Too Many Things

Most children are natural-born collectors—of rocks, marbles, baseball cards, photographs, valentines, their own poems and artwork; you name it. Sometimes these collections get out of control and threaten to take over a shelf or desktop. But that's most often true of such things as poems, artwork, and school papers of various kinds. And even the proudest artist is usually willing to sort through his or her work every couple of months and choose the best for preservation. To tame other accumulations you may simply have to get bigger boxes and bins or perhaps dream up an interesting display idea to show off the items to their best advantage.

But there's no question that sometimes the collections of toys and other paraphernalia have gotten too large and have to be weeded out. Storing certain toys and games—naturally, your child does the choosing—in a carton in a hall closet will not only provide the space needed to help keep the room neat and orderly, it can add new interest and glamour to stored playthings. Some parents cycle toys so only half the toys are even on display. Since deciding which toys to retire is usually difficult because attach-ments grow up around familiar playthings, you might want to schedule this job at the end of the summer when school is just about to begin and new interests abound, or after Christmas, when you have to accommodate a bright new collection.

Working Well with Baby-Sitters

Finding the right baby-sitter can take time and ingenuity but it is so gratifying to have a responsible and capable person to stay with your children that the effort is well worth it. It's important to have a list of several people you've met and can trust, even though you may hire one person on a regular basis, so that you'll be ready when your standby is sick or unavailable. Sometimes colleges and nursing schools have employment offices that will supply likely candidates. A neighborhood teenager or older friend whom you and the children both know might be good prospects. If you don't know a sitter, always check several references before making a decision about whether you want to hire her. Ask about everything that is important to you, because you'll feel more secure later and your children will benefit from this attention to detail.

When you hire a sitter be specific about what you want her to do and also make arrangements for payment and for getting her home. And if there is anything complicated about getting to your house or apartment, remember to point that out.

Baby-Sitter's Book. To make sure that the baby-sitter for a particular evening has all the information you want her to have— information about where you are and how to reach you as well as bedtimes and essential instructions about your children—it's a good idea to start a baby-sitter's book. Use a spiral-bound notebook held open with a rubber band. On the left-hand page (which you'll keep from week to week), write down all permanent information, such as doctor's phone number, poison-control center, and the like. Here's what you should include:

- doctor's name and telephone number
- poison-control center's telephone number
- police emergency number
- fire-department number
- telephone number of grandparents if they live in the same city

• office numbers of you and your husband if you hire daytime sitters

• location of first-aid supplies

• information about night-lights or dimmers required in children's rooms

• how to turn air-conditioner on and off

• where phones are located in the house (You should show all new sitters where these are as well.)

On the right-hand page, you can list all changeable information that relates to that particular day or night. These right-hand pages get torn off after you get home. Date the top of the page and list the telephone number of where you are going to be as well as anything else the sitter will need. Here's what you might want to include:

• name and telephone number of the people you'll be visiting, as well as when you expect to arrive there and when you'll leave

• what kind of snack the children and sitter can have

• which TV programs children are allowed to watch

• important bedtime rituals: favorite stories, songs, etc.

• name and phone number of a nearby friend or neighbor who is going to be home

Ask baby-sitters for additional suggestions and you'll get the benefit of other mothers' accumulated wisdom. Also, remember to take the time to give each new sitter a quick tour of the house so she will know where the entrances are and what she needs to know about the layout of your home.

Keeping Pace with Your Child's Growth

As children grow, their abilities and interests develop and change at a pretty rapid rate. To keep pace with their widening horizons and developing skills, you'll have to do periodic reviews of their environments and their job assignments. How often will depend on your individual situation, but it's important to be aware that such reviews will be necessary. It's also vital to make any significant changes in family life a collaborative effort. Most families find that a full-scale discussion at a family council paves the way for cooperative housekeeping and for any changes that might be disturbing if simply imposed from above. One word of warning about overhasty changes: Sometimes both parents and children are a little too eager to see children grow up. They may decide to get rid of "childish" toys, "babyish" decorations and the like as a sign that a child is growing up. Experience has shown, however, that it's best to put such old favorites in a halfway house rather than to get rid of them entirely, so that they can be easily retrieved if they are missed.

· 10 · | Easy Entertaining and Happy Holidays

Carefree parties and joyous family holidays are two more of the many rewards you'll get from putting your day-to-day activities in order. Which isn't to say that happy celebrations will just happen, without planning and effort on your part. What it does mean is that once you have the essentials of your life under control, you'll find that giving successful parties is a whole lot easier and much more fun than it used to be. Of course, even in our darkest days of disorganization, most of us gave a sprinkling of parties and somehow managed to piece together some sort of holiday festivities. It's just that we did it in the face of such gigantic obstacles that fun wasn't part of the picture. In fact we often actively suffered through what were supposed to be joyful occasions. Well, those days are over. Now that your house is reasonably neat, your kitchen is verging on apple-pie order, and you've learned the secrets of sane scheduling, you're ready to start enjoying the festive occasions of life.

Easy entertaining really is possible. All you need to do is apply your organizational skills once again, give up perfectionism, and choose the kind of party that genuinely suits your temperament, your life-style and your budget. And it means taking the lead from professional cooks and caterers and planning every aspect of your party well in advance—on paper. It could also mean hiring help or buying much or all of the food from a gourmet takeout shop. So if buffets for twenty-four intimate and exhaust you, adjust your sights. Give a soup-and-dessert party for six, a do-ahead brunch for eight (no last-minute omelets at this one), or a make-your-own-hero party for ten. When you do what you're comfortable with, you're relaxed and outgoing, and in that frame of mind, you'll make your guests feel warmly welcome. And that's much more important to real hospitality than dazzling everyone with your cooking skills. In fact, all of us probably have happy memories of parties where the food consisted of a selection of interesting cheeses, good bread, fruit, and wine. And that kind of indoor picnic might be just the place for you to begin. You'll have no pre-party jitters and no pots and pans to scrub when it's over, but you will get back into the swing of entertaining—making the master plan, inviting the guests, seeing that tableware and other equipment are in order and ready. It's the ideal way to launch yourself into easy entertaining.

Using a written master plan will make brunches, suppers, and other simple gatherings much more manageable, and if writing out a checklist is productive even for such easy parties, you can imagine how valuable it will be when you tackle a birthday party for seven seven-year-olds, a Halloween party for four neighborhood kids and their parents, or a baby shower for an expectant mother and ten of her friends. Any time there are decorations, favors, and activities or games to account for, getting it all down in black and white is more useful than ever.

Even more than parties, holidays can get to be intimidating. Just thinking about Thanksgiving and Christmas can strike fear into the hearts of some. Adding all those extra chores to an already busy schedule can seem beyond your capabilities. Yet you can learn to tame holidays if you sit down with pencil and paper, decide what it is you really want, and plan for it. By starting early, assigning small tasks to each day, and keeping your expectations within reasonable limits, you can have the happiest holidays you've had since you were a kid. What's more, you'll usually find your family is much more cooperative in sharing the preparations for celebrations than for day-to-day chores. Why not assign cleanup chores alternately with cookie baking, making decorations, and tree trimming? You just might be in for a pleasant surprise.

Instant-Action Party Plan

One of the great pleasures in life is sharing good food and drink with close friends—if you've learned how to cope with entertainment anxiety. And you will. Since you don't want to stay a recluse until you've got every tiny household detail in pristine order, there's no time like a month from now for giving your first party. It can be a secret celebration of your newfound neatness. Why not an after-dinner dessert party, a Sunday afternoon cheese-and-wine party or a Sunday noon brunch? Whatever you choose, every element of it will be laid out in a master plan: the guest list (check off names after you call), the menu, the shopping list, the nonfood supply list, the bar list, the timetable, even your pre-party cleaning schedule. Don't be tempted to omit any of the elements even though you think writing everything down seems too elaborate for a small simple party. Say you choose an after-dinner dessert party for eight. Your plan should include everything. This is the single most important secret of successful, trouble-free entertaining. Because it allows step-by-step mastery, it keeps you calm and flexible.

To launch you in planning your own party, a sample plan for the after-dinner dessert party follows. Use the same approach for whatever simple party you choose—wine-and-cheese, soup-and-dessert, or what-have-you.

After-Dinner Dessert Party for 8

Budget $30
Guest List:
> Jane and Dan
> Connie and André
> Martha and John
> Susan and Sam

Menu:
>
> Lemon mousse with raspberry sauce (Aunt Mary's recipe)
> Chocolate chocolate-chip cookies (to buy at bakery)
> Brown-sugar pecan shortbread (to make)
> Dark-roast coffee
> Sanka
> Darjeeling tea

Food Shopping List:
>
> Ingredients for mousse:
>> Unflavored gelatin
>> 4 lemons
>> Granulated sugar
>> 1 cup heavy cream (8 oz.)
>> Salt (on hand)
>> 1 dozen eggs
>> 2 10-oz. packages frozen raspberries
>
> Ingredients for brown-sugar pecan shortbread:
>> 1/2 lb. butter
>> 1 lb. light-brown sugar
>> 1 4-oz. can pecans
>> Flour (on hand)
>> Salt (on hand)
>> Baking powder (on hand)
>> Vanilla extract (on hand)
>
> Dark-roast coffee
> Half-and-half (milk and cream)
> Sanka (on hand)
> Darjeeling Tea (on hand)

Nonfood Shopping List:
>
> Coffee filters
> Candles for table
> Flowers at supermarket for table
> Coffee liqueur (optional)

Schedule: Party at 9 o'clock on Saturday night
>
> Invite guests 2 weeks ahead
> Buy nonfood items 1 week before party

Buy food Thursday before party
Make mousse and raspberry sauce Friday night
Bake brown-sugar pecan shortbread Saturday morning
Clean living room and dining area (light cleaning) Saturday
   afternoon
Set table at 7:30 P.M. on Saturday
Set up coffee at 8 P.M. on Saturday
Get out Sanka and tea (at 8:15 P.M.)
Put sugar and half-and-half in sugar bowl and creamer
Put coffee water on at 9:15 P.M.
Make coffee at 9:20 P.M.
Set out cookies at 9:25 P.M.
Serve at 9:30 P.M.

Parties That Please

Once you've given a super-simple party or two and you've en-joyed the warmth and conviviality that relaxed entertaining can bring, you'll probably want to tackle something a bit more chal-lenging and satisfying. But before you do, it might be a good idea to allocate some time to an In-Depth Assessment of both party-giving and holiday observances to decide what will work best for you and your family. This may seem to be a pretty serious ap-proach for a rather lighthearted topic, but anyone who has been involved in the stress and frenzy of poorly planned parties or who has come to dread the sight of the first pumpkin in the markets knows that celebrations gone awry are no laughing matter. To find out what has been going wrong so you can make things right will mean asking yourself some basic questions about your sched-ule, your life-style, and the kind of social life that makes sense for you in terms of your budget, the size of your home, and your tastes. Once again, it's a matter of establishing priorities.

Let's begin by looking at a nonholiday party; we'll review hol-idays in a later section. Very often people get into the habit of en-tertaining in a particular way because their mothers did it or because it worked fine before they had kids and a job. Then, too, a great many people have hidden perfectionistic standards so that they feel guilty about serving a less-than-extraordinary meal; or serving food, no matter how good, that they haven't cooked themselves; or hiring help to tend bar or lend a hand generally. And it's often true that people don't really look at the evidence to discover the kind of parties they genuinely enjoy. Here are some questions for you to consider:

- What kind of parties do you like most to attend?
- What kind of parties have you liked most when you were host?
- What are the parties you gave that you liked least? Why?
- Is your kitchen well equipped for party cooking? What would improve it?
- Is your bar well equipped with glasses, the right liquor for the occasion in the right amounts? Is it conveniently located?
- Do you start your party planning too late, so that you find yourself dashing around and making last-minute trips to the market or liquor store?
- Is menu planning a problem for you? Have you got at least one party-menu cookbook that suits your cooking skills, tastes, and budget?

Review your past party-giving and write down everything that seems important to you. Identify the problems and come up with realistic solutions. If you find that you always take on more than you can comfortably do in the kitchen, start specializing in totally do-ahead meals. No more last-minute cheese puffs for appetizers, no more stir-fried shrimp, no more pasta that goes in the pot after the guests arrive. If you find yourself completely exhausted from your frenzied schedule, do simpler parties, hire help, extend your schedule. After you've analyzed your own feelings and attitudes, talk with your partner about his. Also, set up a family conference to discuss family parties and celebrations, to find out what everyone most enjoys and also to allocate jobs for an upcoming holiday. Often we outdo ourselves at holiday times trying to achieve some fantasy observance that isn't really what anyone in the family wants. And we don't ask for the help we need. Let's look at a full-scale party plan you can use once you've determined the sort of parties you'd like to give.

A Full-Scale Party Plan That Works

If you think of yourself as catering your own parties, you'll find that you've adopted the best approach. Caterers wouldn't dream of using a hit-and-miss method. They write everything down. After you've written out a full-scale party plan you'll see how incredibly valuable it is. As you reread it, you'll notice items you overlooked. Or you'll realize that your menu won't work because you need two different oven temperatures at the same time. Or you'll see that you just don't have time to produce the meal you've selected. Remember, it's no crime to choose easy make-ahead dishes, to buy several dishes at a gourmet food shop, or to serve a dessert as simple as good ice cream with a luscious sauce.

Choosing and inviting your guests. Since the guests are the main ingredient of any party, you'll find writing down a list of people you'd like to see the natural first step in your master plan. Obviously, you'll list old friends, but spend some time thinking about people you've met recently whom you'd like to get to know better. A casual party is the ideal setting for introducing new friends to old ones. And think more about whether people will enjoy each other than about whether they're all the same age or whether you have equal numbers of women and men. After you've got a list—with a few extras to allow for turndowns—you're ready to call or write out invitations. Exactly when you choose to invite your guests will depend partly on the time of year. If it's near the holiday season, you might want to allow three or four weeks between the invitation and the party. Other times, two weeks will probably be long enough. In summer when many people go away on vacation or visit the beach, you may want to start three weeks ahead. Stay flexible and you'll be able to assemble an interesting group.

Setting the budget and choosing the menu. Before you choose a menu, decide about how much you have to spend on the party.

That way, you'll have a pretty good idea of what would be appropriate foods. You'll be aware of whether you can afford steak or chicken, asparagus or broccoli, strawberries or raspberries, and what your choice of wine should be. You'll always have to allow for a bit of leeway, but beginning with a target sum alllows you to allocate amounts to the various courses and drinks so you won't get in over your head. Happily, many do-ahead recipes are also low-cost, so you will get two advantages at once. If you don't have a variety of interesting recipes you can make in advance, check out your cookbooks, ask a knowledgeable friend, or start clipping newspaper and magazine recipes. Do this a month or so before the party, so that you have time to set up a cooking schedule and get comfortable with it.

When you plan a menu, remember that the best meals offer a variety of different tastes, textures, and colors. So if you're going to serve lemon chicken as the main course, you'll want to avoid a lemon-flavored dessert or a lemon salad dressing. If your main course has a tomato sauce, it's best not to use tomatoes in your salad. Study menus in magazines and newspapers to get an idea of the kinds of combinations the professional cooks choose. Also, remember to note whether the dishes you've chosen fit together in terms of the way they are to be prepared or heated.

Making a shopping list. After you've selected the recipes, write them out or photocopy them so that you will have all of them in one place; trying to work with two or three cookbooks in your kitchen can be a real hassle. Next, read through the ingredients list of each recipe you are going to make to see what you have on hand (be sure you have enough of whatever it is) and what you will need to buy. Then write up a party shopping list. Then read through the recipes again to see whether you have the serving pieces you'll need, and get them out and wash them if that's necessary. Make a list of all these items so that on the day of the party you can check it quickly to make sure everything is handy.

Generally, it's a good idea to do the bulk of your food shopping four or five days before the party and then pick up the meat and very perishable items a day or two before.

Stocking the bar. For this particular party—either the brunch or the soup-and-dessert lunch—you'll need only one kind of drink and something nonalcoholic for those guests who don't drink. With the brunch you might plan to serve white sangria or mimosas (a combination of orange juice and champagne), and with the lunch, either beer or wine, depending on the soup you choose. But if you were giving a dinner party or a cocktail party, you'd probably want to check in a bar guide to decide how much to stock for the number of guests you've invited.

Nonfood party supplies. Very often people pay too little attention to stocking these supplies and find that they're missing something important—wineglasses or candles or something else vital. So check napkins, glasses, flatware, china—everything you'll be using—to make sure you're well equipped. And don't forget ashtrays and matches.

A countdown schedule. Once you've got your vital lists written and you've checked equipment, you'll want to make a note about such things as extra ice, where to put the cat, the clothes you're going to wear, where the guests are going to put their coats, flowers or leafy branches for decoration, and all the other details that have to be taken into account. Then you can make a timetable in the form of a Party Countdown Schedule (see sample). This should be tailored to your own special needs, so do add whatever you think will make it most useful. Light housecleaning can be included on this list the weekend before, but do not take on any major cleaning projects right before a party—do not foam-clean your rug, do not wash down the walls of the bathroom, or undertake any other perfectionistic enterprise of this sort. Most people do not notice or care, while other perfectionists will never be satisfied anyway.

Party Countdown Schedule

Three to Four Weeks Ahead

• Decide what type of party you want to give and how much you can spend on it.

- Determine guest list and invite guests if party is in holiday season.
- Arrange for helper, if using one.

Two Weeks Ahead

- Invite guests if nonbusy season.
- Decide on menu, assemble recipes, make shopping list.
- Make bar list.
- Make nonfood party-supply list.
- Review serving pieces, glasses, napkins, other equipment.

One Week Ahead

- Shop for nonperishable supplies and liquor.
- Do weekly housecleaning or hire someone to do it (no major projects).
- Check clothing you will wear.

Five Days Ahead

- Shop for all food, except meat and perishable items.
- Check tissues, bathroom supplies, towels, etc.

Four Days Ahead

- Housecleaning review to make sure entryway, hall closet, bathroom, and living room are all clean.
- Check cooking utensils and equipment.
- Make extra ice and put in plastic bags.

Three Days Ahead

- Prepare any ingredients that need processing (grate cheese, toast and chop nuts). Do any kitchen chores that can be done ahead (store cheese and nuts in plastic bags in refrigerator).

Two Days Ahead

- Check garnishes, flavorings, fill pepper mills, salt shakers, sugar bowls.
- Make dessert.

One Day Ahead
- Make one dish that can be made ahead (soup, quick bread, etc.).
- Wash and dry lettuce, parsley, vegetable garnishes.

Day of Party
- Prepare main course.
- Make salad dressing.
- Set table.
- Chill wine.
- Assemble glasses on tray or set up bar.
- Prepare coffeepot and coffee tray.
- One hour in advance set out any foods that should be served at room temperature (cheese, breads, etc.).
- Review menu and add to this list.

Children's Birthday Parties

As important as Christmas and other holidays are to most children, there's something extra-special about celebrating their own birthdays. Having just the right party to honor the occasion is one of the high points of happy family life. But when anything is that important, planning is essential—as is lots of help, from the experts as well as your friends. Another crucial element to success is to make the birthday boy or girl a consultant on pre-party plans. Young children are not good candidates for surprise parties. They like to be involved and they often have pretty definite ideas about what makes a party good. They can be a tremendous help in guiding your choice of foods, games, and decorations. Of course, not everything they suggest will be usable in exactly the form they suggest it. You may have to negotiate a compromise between inviting the whole circus and inviting one talented teen-aged clown, and between taking the whole class skating and taking three or four good friends to the rink. The point is that such consultation will make it much more likely that the party you give will please the person it's meant to please.

What more can you do? Well, the people who are in the party business—who've worked out hundreds of different master plans for successful children's parties—say you should start with five factors in mind:

- The interests and tastes of the guest of honor, which we've just discussed
- The space available
- Your budget
- The age and number of guests
- The time of year

The party professionals also recommend that you attend one or two children's parties before you give your first one. Happily, that's very easy to do, because most mothers will eagerly welcome an adult volunteer who can help with serving the refreshments, overseeing the games and generally lending support and willing hands. Once you've attended a few parties as an observer, you'll have a much better idea of how to pace activities, what games work best, and where the trouble spots are likely to be.

All the mothers I consulted were unanimous on the subject of prizes—they felt there should be one for every guest. Also, they suggested keeping competitive games to a minimum since such games can be a source of trouble and tears. Another recommendation of the old-hand party givers was to make sure that you serve the ice cream and cake right after the presents are opened because that tends to soften the blow children experience when giving up a desirable toy as a present. Finally, everybody says to keep parties for children short, no more than two hours or so. And make sure all parents know when to pick up their children.

Since some activities click at one party and not at another, it's a good idea to have about twice as many as you think you'll need. Ask your children and other mothers for suggestions or look for books on the subject at your local public library.

Of all the forms of party-giving, celebrating a child's birthday successfully is one of the most gratifying; so focus on the rewards, plan carefully, and you should have a wonderful time.

Heartwarming Holidays

With sound planning your holidays can be times of family close-ness and fun, generous hospitality and a choice array of good things to eat and drink. If holiday celebrations haven't been sat-isfying recently, it's time to take stock and apply the In-Depth Assessment techniques so that you can set things to rights. You don't have to resign yourself to high stress, short tempers, and disappointment. Because holidays tend to be laden with great ex-pectations (often unrealistic ones) and considerable emotional weight, it's sometimes hard to sort out all the elements, ques-tions, and problems until we do a written assessment. Attempt-ing too much and poor scheduling tactics are two common problems that may not be apparent until we write down all that we're trying to do and see how overbooked we are. Other issues will emerge as you proceed. So you'll be able to evaluate your own feelings and priorities before you discuss the subject with your husband and children. To begin, ask yourself pretty much the same questions you asked about parties, but add anything about the holiday that strikes you as significant. Here's a sampling to get you started:

• What are the most important aspects of the holiday to you? Have you gotten away from those recently?

• What did you value and enjoy most about successful celebra-tions in the past?

• What do you think has gone wrong with the celebrations that you didn't enjoy?

• How can you eliminate stressful and unsatisfying elements from future celebrations?

• What would you like to add to enrich the holiday? More family activities? Music and other traditional activities?

• Do you want to introduce more quiet times?

• When should you start planning for each holiday? What hol-iday activities are most important to you and your family? Often little things matter a lot more than we might expect, so it's a good idea to discuss every holiday well in advance at a family conference. Since traditions add richness and excitement to our festive occasions, you might want to do a bit of research into the ways people in other countries and at other times have celebrated special days. Children and adults both enjoy active planning and participation more than just passively waiting for the next TV special or community event. Public libraries have all sorts of books that might contribute delightful ideas for your own family celebrations, including holiday cookbooks.

In this book I'm just going to touch on a few holiday highlights that have come up in interviews with some of the busy mothers I've talked with. Establishing your own holiday traditions is something you and your family will have a lot of fun doing on your own. Like everything else, happy holidays take planning and organization, but always allow room for spur-of-the-moment pleasures.

Happy Halloween

Most children love to dress up as a favorite character and they often start planning what they are going to be for Halloween long before the day. And they love the jack-o'-lanterns, ghosts, and witches that are the symbols of this day. But in recent years Halloween celebrations have had to be redirected because of scares involving poisoned or polluted treats. So make sure that your children only go trick-or-treating at nearby neighbors' houses (always accompanied by an adult), and then plan a Halloween party with neighborhood mothers to show off costumes, bob for apples, and tell ghost stories, and perhaps have hot dogs or other sandwiches. There's no reason that this new way of celebrating shouldn't be just as much fun as the old ways. Plan costumes and the festivities early enough, and all will go smoothly as well as safely.

How to Be Thankful for Thanksgiving

To some people the arrival of Thanksgiving signals a time of sharing and festive celebration, to others it introduces the frantic season. And there's no doubt that getting all that bounty on the table requires sound planning. One great way to make the holiday a pleasure for the whole family is to involve everyone in preparations. Children enjoy Thanksgiving much more when they can help with the cooking and table decorations and offer ideas for making the house look festive. Guests are usually delighted to bring a favorite family dish to enhance your table. When you make the meal a cooperative venture, everybody has the pleasure of sharing and no one gets burdened with too much to do. But you will need to make your master plan early.

Traditional Thanksgiving menus from days gone by were often very elaborate and too heavy for today's appetites. It's no longer necessary to begin the meal with soup, prepare six vegetable dishes, and offer three kinds of pie. So keep the food festive and delectable but don't think that you have to provide exactly the same meal your grandmother used to serve.

Treat holiday dinners just as you would any other party meal and make a master plan at least two weeks in advance so that you can stock up on nonfood and nonperishable items well before the big day. Then buy your turkey, vegetables, and salad makings closer to Thanksgiving. Last-minute shopping on Wednesday is a mistake for two reasons—it heightens anxiety, and you often can't find the right brand or size turkey you want without time-consuming visits to three or more supermarkets. Another benefit of the written plan is that it lets you assign do-ahead dishes to guests or make them with the help of your family. Here again as in the party plan, list everything, including the makings of your centerpiece. Be thrifty and choose a table decoration made up of fruits, nuts, and vegetables you'll eat later. Ears of Indian corn make an interesting addition. The weekend before Thanksgiving, write out a countdown timetable for the holiday, taking all aspects of your celebration into consideration. List the menu, the cooking times for those dishes you are preparing, tableware and serving pieces, choice of napkins and candles and whether candlesticks need to be washed or polished, when you want to assemble cold dishes—everything. With this kind of planning, even a meal for twenty can be manageable and will make this year's celebration one you're genuinely thankful for.

Christmas Is Coming

The Christmas season is a favorite time of year for many people, but it's a demanding time that cries out for organization. To have a happy, satisfying holiday, start your planning the weekend before the first of December. Of course, you'll want to start even earlier for gift buying, especially if you're sending gifts overseas. But with these exceptions, you can get all your activities accomplished by distributing them over a December calendar. You can make a family calendar with bright-colored felt-tipped pens or you can simply use the family calendar in the kitchen. (See the Christmas Activity Checklist below.)

Begin your Christmas planning by making a list of everything you want to do. Don't overdo but don't eliminate things that you genuinely enjoy. The whole point of planning is to give some thought to what your priorities are and come to terms with any streak of perfectionism that may be at the root of a too-busy schedule. Sit down and think about the kind of holiday you'd actually like to have, then discuss it with your family. Of course, one aspect of sitting down and making a plan may mean facing the fact that you have less money to spend than you'd like. However, once you've looked that reality boldly in the eye, you will be much better equipped to think of creative ways of solving your financial dilemma. You'll soon find that you come up with some of your best gift ideas—delectable gifts from your kitchen, specialty books from the discount shelves, posters from a nearby museum, sporting goods from a discount catalog, pottery mugs from a school crafts fair.

If you just can't seem to get into the right frame of mind for Christmas planning, put on a record or tape of your favorite Christmas music and take down a copy of *A Christmas Carol* by Charles Dickens.

Christmas Activity Checklist

Budget for remaining gifts and cards

Make a gift list

Buy wrapping paper and ribbon

Buy gifts for out-of-towners

Make Christmas card list

Wrap and mail gifts to out-of-towners (November after Thanksgiving)

Buy stamps for cards

Address and mail cards (two weeks before Christmas)

Buy gifts for family and friends in town (Be sure to start early)

Decide on holiday activities and decorations for house at family conference

Plan and write out holiday menu

Christmas baking (make a plan)

Buy tree and other greens

Trim the tree

Wrap gifts for family and friends

Holiday concerts, school pageants, plays, family activities

To keep your schedule sensible and your stress level to a minimum, remember that it's usually the simplest pleasures we remember longest. Christmas time is a time to enjoy your family and to share cherished rituals—special foods, special music, baking and cooking together, and giving pleasure to others. So focus on activities that reflect the spirit of the season, plan your time with care and enjoy the beauty of simple rituals and sharing.

This has been a year to remember. The year you got organized!

Index